COOK
YOUR
WAY
THIN

COOK
YOUR
WAY
THIN

By Ethel K. Feldman

AN
ARC
BOOK

ARCO PUBLISHING COMPANY, INC.
219 Park Avenue South, New York, N.Y. 10003

Second Printing, 1974

An ARC Book
Published 1973 by Arco Publishing Company, Inc.
219 Park Avenue South, New York, N.Y. 10003

Library of Congress Catalog Card Number 72-96288

ISBN 0-668-02942-0

Printed in the United States of America

Foreword

If you've already plunked down your money to buy this book, you take your dieting seriously. You're either a member or alumnus of one of the leading diet clubs and **you know the rules**.

I first started dieting when I was 14 years old. There's very little I don't know about eating . . . overeating . . . crash dieting . . . starving . . . gorging myself . . . the whole depressing cycle. In all, I estimate that I've lost and gained almost 1,500 pounds. And probably so have you.

My story is not so unique. Seven years ago, after a lifetime of obesity, I joined a local diet group. Not only did I lose 60 pounds, but my creative cooking urges were redirected into my own brand of "low calorie cookery" which, I'm told, has made gourmet cooking easy and controlled eating a pleasure.

This book is a collection of my personal favorite recipes. Anyone can make them and anyone can eat them! Also, this book may be useful to those of you with health problems other than obesity. You might wish to get your Doctor's approval before cooking this **high-protein, low-fat** way.

You will be amazed to find that many of these low calorie recipes have the look and taste of gourmet dishes. You will also discover the art of improvising—combining some old, some new—the best of each **for you** . . . creating your own style and learning the joy of **cooking your way thin**.

Acknowledgments

Cook Your Way Thin, my labor of love, has been seven years in the writing. It goes without saying that it would never have been started without the inspiration of a local diet group, where I lost 60 pounds and learned the "discipline" of controlled eating.

I owe much to so many, too numerous to mention. Here are just a few without whose help there would be no book: Elaine Feldman, who has edited, assembled, and typed **Cook Your Way Thin**; Diana Dean was my guiding light in getting this project off the ground. Her know-how and professional advice are reflected in the pages of this book, and I am deeply indebted to her; warm thanks to Joan Walker, Director of the New Way of Life Weight Control Centers and broadcaster of the "Keeping Slender" radio program in Stamford, Connecticut. Joan's confidence in my cooking ability and her invitations to do food demonstrations for her diet groups mean more than I can say; my affection to Anne Kramer Scherer, owner of the "New You" diet groups in Fairfield County, Connecticut, for her strong belief that my cookbook is a "must" for dieters; and more thanks to the loyal ladies of my "Low Calorie Kitchen" cooking classes who've tested, enjoyed, and proven that it really **works**.

And finally . . . heartfelt gratitude to the hundreds of dieters in the Fairfield County area who encouraged me, inspired me, and never stopped clamoring for my recipes to be put into book form.

Here they are! Eat . . . and again, you will **Cook Your Way Thin!**

Contents

COOK
YOUR
WAY
THIN

Helpful Cooking Hints and Terms

1. How to reconstitute powdered milk? Place 1/3 cup of powdered milk in a measuring cup, fill to 8 ozs. with water, and stir well . . . or, follow package directions

2. In the use of salt, my preference is for coarse kosher salt. Regular table salt is interchangeable in my recipes, but if you use it, please keep the measurements scant.

3. To "score" a cucumber, run the tines of a fork from top to bottom of the cucumber. This makes attractive slices for decorating platters.

4. To "toast" sesame seeds, place them in a small skillet, continually moving it back and forth over a low flame on top of the stove. The seeds will become slightly browned and you may hear a popping noise.

5. Reference is made to "cooked-down" tomato juice in many of my recipes. All you do is simmer the juice in an uncovered pan until it is reduced by half.

6. To "simmer" on top of the stove is to allow the food to cook on the lowest heat, which will produce small bubbles.

7. To "french-cut" string beans, cut off the ends of the beans and then cut through the rounded side. Cook them fresh . . . you will find it difficult to use canned french-cut beans after that! And try

9

"frenching" waxed beans—an unlimited vegetable.

8. A pepper mill is a must! Nothing enhances the flavor of cooking like freshly ground pepper.

9. Dehydrated onion and vegetable flakes may be reconstituted by allowing them to soak in a little water. Use about 2-3 tbsps. of water to 1 tbsp. of dried flakes for about 5 minutes. (This is why dehydrated onion and vegetable flakes thicken any liquid to which they are added.)

10. Summer squashes are usually of the soft skin variety. Yellow, zucchini, and other summer squashes are unlimited vegetables. Winter squashes are of the hard-shell variety—butternut, acorn—and are to be used at dinner meals only, in 4-oz. portions.

11. Clean fresh mushrooms by wiping with a damp cloth. If mushrooms are very dirty, wash them under cold, running water, and dry well. Cut off a small slice from the bottoms of the mushrooms. To slice them, cut down from top to bottom, thus retaining the shape of the mushroom.

12. "Browning" chicken for a special recipe? Just broil for a few minutes to achieve the "browned" color and then proceed with the recipe.

13. Keep a shaker jar of cinnamon and Sweet 'N Low mixed together. Fill a measuring cup with 1/3 cinnamon and 2/3 Sweet 'N Low. This combination is used in many of my recipes. You may adjust the mixture to your own taste by adding more sweetener to the cinnamon.

14. Make up the Cranberry Conserve (p. 158) and keep it on hand in the refrigerator. It will stay fresh for weeks and is very good on toast.

15. You can also keep a supply of Baked Apples on

hand, enough for a week (refrigerated, of course). I bake 12 at a time because my family enjoys them, too!

16. At the end of the summer season, when peaches are inexpensive, buy and freeze them to have on hand for making ice cream over the winter months. Peel and slice each peach. Then place the slices on Saran Wrap and flatten the packet gently with your hand. Freeze the packets individually and, after they are frozen, put them all in a plastic bag, securing it with a tie. This will keep for many months!

17. Keep 4-oz. portions of evaporated skimmed milk frozen by pouring it into a paper cup and freezing solid. In your freezer you can keep this for several weeks. This, then will be on hand for ice cream and desserts.

18. Store a small stainless steel mixing bowl and beaters in your freezer. You'll always know where they are and they will be chilled and ready for use.

19. Blueberries can be frozen by washing and drying carefully. Place them on a flat tray to freeze. When they are frozen, transfer them to a plastic bag and secure with a tie.

20. Here's one for a mathematician: milk computations! The daily milk allowance is 2 cups of skimmed milk (reconstituted from powdered milk) or buttermilk, or 1 cup of evaporated skimmed milk. For each ounce of evaporated skimmed milk, deduct 2 ozs. from your daily allowance if you use your milk in liquid form.

21. For a simple and filling fish lunch (my favorites are Clam Chowder (p. 38) or any of the fish soups), refer to the "Fish and Shellfish" section (p. 87). Since

you will be eating five fish meals weekly, vary your menu by the use of hearty fish soups!

22. Reference to powdered skimmed milk in this book means to use the milk in dry form. If there is a need for the milk to be used in liquid form, the directions will so state.

23. When a recipe calls for a small can of mushrooms, use the 4-oz. size.

24. Do you want to make a sandwich . . .dieter's style? Simply toast one slice of enriched white bread. As soon as it is toasted, slice through the middle, making two thin slices. Wrap in Saran Wrap. Always carry your sandwich filling and lettuce separetely in Saran Wrap or a container, and put the sandwich together at lunch time.

25. At this writing, as you know, the cyclamate sweeteners are banned by the United States Government. Food flavors will improve after refrigerating when using the new sweeteners!

26. Some of the equipment you will need to keep on hand are:
    General Electric Toaster Oven
    Teflon skillets and junior Loaf Pans
        (7⅜" x 3⅝" x 2¼")
    spatulas
    blender
    small stainless steel mixing bowl
    hand mixer, or a stationary model

27. To eliminate fish odors in your kitchen, dice a stalk of celery (including the leaves) and cook in a separate pot, uncovered, on top of the stove.

28. To dry out basil leaves or Italian parsley (fresh, of course), place uncovered in a 200° oven until dry. Then crumble and place in an air tight jar.

Author's Preferred Products List

Name of Product	Address of Manufacturer or Supplier
Caraway Muenster Cheese	Daitch Shopwell markets, Connecticut and New York
Carnation Instant Non Fat Dry Milk	Most supermarkets
Cheeri Aid (powdered mix for drinks)	A&P brand
Clamato Juice	Most supermarkets
Cott's Diet Soda	Most supermarkets
Ehler's Sauté Onion Powder	Most supermarkets
Extracts and Flavorings: Wagner's, Ehlers or Durkee's	Most food stores, specialty markets, or R.H. Macy
Good Seasons Low-Calorie Italian Dressing	Most supermarkets
KikkoMan Soy Sauce	Most supermarkets
Knox Unflavored Gelatine	Most supermarkets

Kool-Aid	Most supermarkets
MBT Broths	Most supermarkets
McCormick's Season-All Powder	Most supermarkets
Polaner's Deli Salad	Most supermarkets
ReaLemon Reconstituted Lemon Juice	Most supermarkets
Sacramento Tomato Juice	Most supermarkets
Spice Islands White Wine Vinegar and Basil	Most supermarkets
Sweet 'N Low (comes in envelopes and ½-lb. packages)	Most supermarkets
Veal "ham" and smoked veal "sausage" Fresh "veal sausage"	Produced by special request at most quality meat markets

NOTE: Unless a particular brand name is mentioned in the recipe, measurements are for products listed here.

Appetizers

Your mode of entertaining will determine whether you care to use appetizers. For a sit-down dinner, try Steamed Artichokes with Seafood Cocktail Sauce as a first course. You'll wind up giving instructions on how to eat an artichoke!

Raw vegetables and a dip can be used on the hors d'oeuvre table for dieters and non-dieters alike. Try stuffing celery stalks with roasted peppers and season them with McCormick's Season-All Powder.

Use 2 ozs. of Chopped Liver (pp. 68-69) on a bed of lettuce as a first course. Follow this with a 4-oz. serving of Liver, Onions, and Mushrooms (p. 69).

If your main course is to be veal, certainly serve 2 ozs. of Veal Balls in Ginger Ale Sauce first. Then you can use your balance of veal allowance for your main course. I defy the non-dieters to distinguish this from meat balls made of beef!

STEAMED ARTICHOKES WITH COCKTAIL SAUCE

Trim tips of leaves with scissors. Cut off 1″ from the top of the artichoke; then, cut the bottom of the artichoke so that it will stand. Steam in a covered pan,

15

allowing 1½″ of water on the bottom of the pan, for about 40 minutes. Artichoke will be cooked when a leaf pulls out easily. Turn the artichoke over to drain.

Dip the leaves, stem end, in Seafood Cocktail Sauce (p. 147). Place stem end between your teeth and pull the bottom part through . . . gently. When you get to the "choke" (after all the leaves have been eaten), pare off with a knife and eat the bottom of the artichoke dipped in the sauce.

This is my very favorite appetizer! Remember . . . one artichoke is equal to a limited dinner vegetable.

VEAL BALLS IN GINGER ALE SAUCE

1 qt. diet ginger ale
3 cups tomato juice
2 lbs. ground veal
2 tbsps. dried onion flakes
1½ tsps. salt
¼ tsp. pepper
½ tsp. garlic powder
1 tbsp. Italian parsley or
　　1 tsp. parsley flakes
½ cup water

Simmer tomato juice and ginger ale, uncovered, while working on the rest of this recipe. Mix meat with all of the other ingredients, and form into meatballs. Brown in a Teflon pan. After the meatballs have browned, add them to the ginger ale-tomato juice mixture and simmer, uncovered, for about 1½ hours, or until the sauce is reduced and very thick. (This freezes very well.)

As an appetizer at dinner, serve 2 ozs. and follow with a 4-oz. dinner portion of any of my veal dishes. Serve this to guests; they'll surely ask for the recipe.

DIP FOR RAW VEGETABLES

1 cup buttermilk
1 tbsp. and 1 tsp. of Good Seasons
    Low-Calorie Italian Dressing
Several sprinkles of garlic powder

Combine the ingredients and shake immediately. Garnish with cut-up fresh chives or freeze-dried chives and refrigerate to thicken. This is excellent with cut-up raw cauliflower, cucumbers, celery, broccoli and green and red peppers!

VEAL BALLS IN SPAGHETTI SAUCE

Veal Ball Mixture
1 lb. raw ground veal
1 tsp. of salt
¼ tsp. of garlic powder
Several sprinkles of pepper
4 ozs. cooked-down tomato
    juice (reduced from 8 ozs.)
1½ tbsps. of dried onion flakes

Sauce Mixture
4 oz. can of mushrooms (reserve liquid)
Several ounces of water
8 ozs. of cooked-down tomato juice
(reduced from 16 ozs.)
1 tbsp. of onion flakes
Sprinkle of black pepper
Several sprinkles of garlic powder
8 ozs. of evaporated skimmed milk
1 tsp. of Worcestershire Sauce
Salt to taste (add after cooking, if desired)
2 tbsps. of lemon juice

Meat Directions
Mix all the ingredients together and form into 1-oz.
balls. Brown well in an uncovered Teflon skillet.

Sauce and Finishing Directions
Add the drained mushrooms and ½ cup of liquid
(mushroom juice and water), cooked-down tomato
juice, Worcestershire Sauce, pepper, garlic powder,
dried onion flakes to the browned veal balls. Simmer,
covered, for about 10 to 15 minutes; then add
evaporated skimmed milk and stir well. Add lemon
juice and mix well. Turn the heat off and check to see if
salt is needed.

As a dinner appetizer, you may serve 2 ozs. and
follow with a 4-oz. portion of any of my veal dishes.
Remember that each dinner portion equals ½ of your
daily milk allowance and **all** of your daily tomato juice
allowance.

This is really delicious and can easily be made in
larger amounts for parties. You need not tell anyone it
is dieter's food!

STUFFED CABBAGE

Veal Mixture
2 lbs. ground veal
1½ tsps. salt
⅛ tsp. pepper
4 ozs. tomato juice
1 tbsp. dried onion flakes
¼ tsp. garlic powder

Cabbage and Topping
1 large cabbage
1-lb. can of sauerkraut
1½ to 2 cups of tomato juice
2-3 ozs. of lemon juice
6 envelopes of Sweet 'N Low
   (or more, to taste)

Combine veal mixture and allow to stand while preparing the rest of this recipe. Cut out the core of the cabbage with a sharp knife. Bring a large pot of water to a boil and simmer the cabbage for about five minutes, or until the leaves can be taken apart. Cut part of the top thick vein at the core side off so that you will be able to roll the cabbage after stuffing. Weigh the veal in ½- or 1-oz. portions, depending on your plan for use. (Use larger outer leaves to stuff 1-oz. portions which can be used for meal time, and use smaller leaves to roll ½-oz. portions to be used for appetizers.)

Place veal portion on inside of leaf at core end, and fold over sides of cabbage, forming it into a roll. Place cabbage rolls on the bottom of a roasting pan, open side down. Cover with sauerkraut. Pour tomato juice and lemon juice over the sauerkraut. Bake in a covered pan at 350° for 1½ to 1¾ hours; then, uncover the pan.

Sprinkle Sweet 'N Low into the pan juices and baste well.

Bake uncovered for 30 minutes longer, basting several times. You may want to add about 4 ozs. more of tomato juice if the liquid cooks down too much. (This freezes very well.)

As an appetizer, serve 2-oz. portions. Supplement this with a 4-oz. portion of Veal for the main course.

STUFFED MUSHROOMS

1 dozen large mushrooms
2 tsps. fresh or frozen chives
⅛ tsp. freeze-dried shallots (optional)
Salt and pepper to taste
1½ tbsps. Parmesan cheese

Separate the stems from the caps. Steam both for about 2 to 3 minutes. Drain. Chop stems and add chives, shallots, salt, pepper and cheese. Stuff the mushroom caps, and broil until the cheese melts and the tops brown.

Although mushrooms are an unlimited vegetable and can usually be enjoyed at any time of the day, you will have to limit your consumption of these because of the amount of cheese used.

CELERY STUFFED WITH ROSY COTTAGE CHEESE

4 stalks of celery
4 ozs. of cottage cheese
⅛ to ¼ tsp. of salt

Sprinkles of pepper, garlic powder
   and Sweet 'N Low
1 tsp. red horseradish
⅛ tsp. of poultry seasoning
¼ tsp. dry mustard
1 tbsp. of fresh chives, cut up, or
   1 tsp. of freeze-dried chives
Several tbsps. of liquified milk (optional)

Mix all the ingredients together except the celery and refrigerate for at least ten minutes for the flavors to blend.

Stuff the celery with the mixture and cut into 1½″ pieces. This goes well with tomato juice or any of the cold soups in this book.

Remember to count the cottage cheese as part of your lunch protein; use a cottage cheese dish to complete lunch.

TOMATO JUICE COCKTAIL

1 46-oz. can of Sacramento Tomato Juice
½ envelope of Sweet 'N Low
1 tsp. of salt
1 bay leaf
2 cloves
1 slice of onion, or 1 tsp. of onion flakes
1 stalk of celery, broken up
½ tsp. of parsley
½ tsp. of basil
2 tsps. of vinegar

Simmer all of the ingredients, except the sweetener, for 5 minutes. Strain. Add the sweetener and refrigerate. (This can also be served warm!)

Be sure to count the tomato juice toward your daily allowance.

"LEGAL" ANTIPASTO

Lettuce leaves
Tomato wedges
Pimientos
Roasted peppers
Pickled cucumbers (p. 117)
Marinated Mushrooms (pp. 23-24)
Progresso Eggplant in Vinegar
Celery sticks
Steamed Italian Peppers (optional; pp. 120-121)

Spread lettuce leaves on large serving platter. Arrange wedges of tomatoes, Steamed Italian Peppers, sliced pimientos, roasted peppers, Pickled Cucumbers, Marinated Mushrooms and celery sticks on the bed of lettuce. Add sweetener to the eggplant, to taste; then add the eggplant to the platter. Serve with Wine Vinegar Salad Dressing (p. 142).

Count tomatoes and eggplant as limited dinner vegetables (4-oz. servings).

FRESH MUSHROOM COCKTAIL

1 lb. large fresh mushrooms
Lemon juice
Seafood Cocktail Sauce (p. 147)
Lettuce leaves
Diced celery (optional)

Clean mushrooms and slice down through the mushrooms to make attractive slices. Dip each slice in lemon juice, and drain. Serve on a bed of lettuce and add diced celery. Dip in Seafood Cocktail Sauce.

Seafood Cocktail Sauce contains tomato juice which must be considered in the day's allowance. This recipe is considered an unlimited vegetable.

MARINATED MUSHROOMS #1

1 lb. small mushrooms
¼ cup water
¼ cup white vinegar
½ tsp. dill seeds
1 bay leaf
6 whole black peppercorns
4 whole cloves
1 one-inch stick cinnamon

Wash mushrooms and cut off ends of stems. Place all the ingredients in a saucepan and bring to a boil; then, cook over low heat for five minutes. Pour into a pint jar. Cover tightly and store in the refrigerator.

This is an unlimited vegetable.

MARINATED MUSHROOMS #2

1 lb. fresh mushrooms, sliced
2 to 3 cups of water
Wine vinegar
Accent (optional)
½ tsp. of salt
Sprinkles of pepper
Sprinkles of garlic powder

⅛ tsp. of oregano
Sweetener to taste (start with ½ envelope of Sweet 'N Low)
2 ozs. of lemon juice

Wipe mushrooms with damp cloth (or, if very dirty, wash in cold water and drain).

Bring 2 to 3 cups of water to a boil. Add mushrooms and cook for 1 to 2 minutes. Drain and allow mushrooms to cool.

Fill jar 1/3 to 1/2 full with wine vinegar. Add all of the other ingredients and refrigerate for 1 to 2 hours.

This is an unlimited vegetable.

EGGPLANT CAVIAR

1 large eggplant
4 ozs. or more of water
2 green peppers, diced fine
1 garlic clove, diced fine
1 large onion, diced fine
2 tbsps. white wine vinegar
8 tbsps. cooked-down tomato juice (p. 9)
1 tsp. salt
Sprinkles of pepper
Pinches of Sweet 'N Low (up to ½ envelope)

Bake eggplant for about ¾ to 1 hour. Allow to cool. Peel eggplant and chop into small pieces.

While eggplant is baking, place diced peppers, onions and garlic clove in a Teflon skillet. Add water and cook slowly, uncovered, until vegetables are tender. Add vinegar, tomato juice, salt and pepper, and simmer for a few minutes longer. Add sweetener and eggplant and cook for one or two minutes longer. Refrigerate and serve cold with celery sticks or cucumber slices.

This can be used as an accompaniment to a dinner meal, and stays well in the refrigerator for several days. Weigh off about 6 ozs. for dinner vegetable portion since green peppers are unlimited. Count tomato juice as part of your daily allowance.

MOCK SOUR CREAM DIP

1 oz. of cold water
½ to 1 tsp. of unflavored Knox Gelatin
  (if you prefer this thicker, use 1 tsp.)
7 ozs. of buttermilk
½ tsp. dried onion flakes
½ tsp. of McCormick's Season-All
Sprinkle of garlic powder
Sprinkle of pepper
Pinch or two of sweetener

Soften the gelatin in cold water; then bring to a boil. Allow to cool. Add all of the other ingredients and refrigerate.

Remember to count the buttermilk or tomato juice (see below) toward your daily allowance.

Variation: You can use this as a salad dressing if you add tomato juice and place in the blender. Use about 4 ozs.

CEIL'S ROASTED PEPPERS

2 red peppers
2 green peppers

1 tsp. distilled vinegar
¼ to ½ tsp. of oregano
¼ to ½ tsp. of salt
2 to 3 garlic cloves, or ½ tsp. of garlic powder
Several pinches to ½ envelope of Sweet 'N Low

Cut peppers in half and remove seeds. Place in a shallow pan or pie plate and cover. Bake in 350° oven for 25 minutes; then, pour off liquid and reserve. Uncover pan and broil skin side up for a few minutes so that skin can be removed easily. After skin has been removed, place in shallow pan and allow to cool. Mix all other ingredients listed with the liquid from the baked peppers and pour over the peppers. Cover pan and refrigerate.

This should have a good spicy, garlic flavor. If you do not care for the fresh garlic flavor, substitute garlic powder.

After eating the peppers, reserve the marinade and use with string beans or sliced cucumbers. This will stay for three or four days in the refrigerator.

This is an unlimited vegetable.

NOTE: You can add all of the same ingredients to a can of roasted peppers, using the liquid in the can. This is good ... but the **fresh** peppers are really great!

VEAL SLICES WITH MELON

¼ cantaloupe, sliced
Veal "ham" (See p. 14)

Wrap slice of melon with the ham and secure with a toothpick. Bake at 400° for five to seven minutes. Be sure to weigh the protein!

This counts as half of one fruit, and this recipe is to precede a veal meal only!

BROILED VEAL "PENNIES"

12 ozs. smoked veal "sausage" (See p. 14)

Slice sausage in ¼" slices (round) and broil for a few minutes until well heated through and slightly browned. Serve with dill pickle slices.

This appetizer can be followed by 4 ozs. of any veal dish for a main course at dinner.

NOTE: Since the veal has been smoked, it will not shrink. In using this type of veal, actual weight is considered "cooked" weight.

BLENDER CHOPPED LIVER

8 ozs. beef or chicken liver
  (or, a combination of both)
1 tbsp. dried onion flakes
Sprinkles of pepper and garlic powder
4 ozs. of water
¼ tsp. dried onion flakes (optional)

Cut the liver into small pieces (one half, if chicken livers are used) and cook with all of the other ingredients, except the last ¼ tsp. of onion flakes, in an uncovered pan until the liver is no longer pink.

There should be several tablespoons of liquid left. Place the livers, liquid and cooked onion flakes in a blender. With the blender on low speed, run for a few seconds. Stop the machine and mix contents with a

spatula. Then, run the machine again, stopping to
move the livers around with the spatula. Continue until
the mixture is smooth but not soupy. Add ¼ tsp. of
onion flakes and refrigerate.

Serves 1 for dinner.

This freezes well if you want to double the recipe.
Blend one recipe at a time, however, since it would be
difficult to do more than 8 ozs. of livers.

If you use this as an appetizer, the balance of the
meal's protein should be liver.

Soups

Cold in the summer and hot in the winter . . . let that be your soup guide. When serving fish for dinner, start your meal with a hearty soup.

In the event that you prefer soup as a main course, try any one of the fish soups for a filling luncheon. My favorite fish luncheon is Clam Chowder (p. 38). Add a slice of toast, a beverage, and it's speedy, hot and delicious!

CHINESE VEGETABLE SOUP

4 to 5 envelopes MBT Chicken Broth
24 ozs. of water
4-oz. can of mushrooms, including liquid
6 to 8 stalks of Chinese celery cabbage
Chinese bean sprouts (fresh, if possible)
Cooked french-cut string beans

Bring water and liquid from the mushrooms to a boil and add the MBT Broth. Cut up Chinese cabbage into 1-inch pieces and add to liquid. Simmer for one minute only. Add mushrooms, string beans and bean sprouts, and serve immediately. Do not allow vegetables to become limp. Serves 6.

Optional: You may also add cooked, drained, chopped spinach.

This is a free, unlimited soup, and may be kept in the refrigerator for several days. It can also be frozen if you don't mind the vegetables being a little limp.

ASPARAGUS SOUP

1 can of asparagus (14¼ oz.), cut up, including liquid
1 envelope MBT Vegetable Broth
1 tbsp. dried onion flakes
Salt and pepper to taste

Place all of the ingredients in a blender; then heat. If soup is a little thick, add a little water.

This is unlimited.

NOTE: To make Cream of Asparagus Soup, add 2 to 3 tbsps. of powdered milk when mixing in the blender. Remember to count the milk toward your daily allowance.

TOMATO SOUP

8 ozs. tomato juice
1 tbsp. onion flakes, crumbled
1 tbsp. chives or parsley flakes
½ envelope of Sweet 'N Low

Bring all of the above ingredients to a boil and cook for three to four minutes. Serve.

Count this as part of your daily tomato juice allowance.

MOCK CLAM CHOWDER

32 ozs. tomato juice

32 ozs. of clam juice
4 to 5 tbsps. dried vegetable flakes
4 to 5 tbsps. dried onion flakes
Several sprinkles of freshly ground pepper
Several good sprinkles of thyme
Sweetener to taste (about 2 envelopes of Sweet 'N Low)

Cook all of the above ingredients, except the sweetener, uncovered until the dry vegetables are soft and the soup is thickened. This should be about five minutes or so. Add the sweetener.

This freezes very well and will serve six to eight people. You can also keep it refrigerated for several days.

TOMATO BOUILLON

1 cup tomato juice
1 cup MBT Beef Broth
½ tsp. onion flakes
Salt and pepper to taste
½ bay leaf
1 whole clove
½ rib celery, diced
Sweetener, to taste

Combine all of the above ingredients and simmer for about 15 minutes.

Remember to count the tomato juice as part of your daily allowance.

SQUASH SOUP

1 lb. zucchini squash
2 cups of tomato juice

2 cups of water
1 tbsp. salt
2 tbsps. dried onion flakes
2 stalks of celery, diced
Several shakes of freshly ground pepper
Several good shakes of garlic powder
2 to 3 envelopes of Sweet 'N Low

Cook all of the above ingredients, except the sweetener, in a covered pot for about 50 to 60 minutes. Add sweetener to taste. If soup is too thick for your taste, add a small amount of boiling water to get the consistency you prefer.

This recipe will serve four to six, and will stay well either in the refrigerator or freezer.

DOUBLE STRENGTH CHICKEN SOUP

3 chicken breasts, skin removed
4 cups water
3 envelopes MBT Chicken Broth
3 to 4 stalks celery, cut up
Dried onion flakes (optional)

Bring all of the above ingredients to a boil. Simmer, covered, gently for about one hour. If the onion flakes are used, strain the soup. Refrigerate for an hour; then, skim off the fat.

This recipe will serve four.

TOMATO-ASPARAGUS SOUP

16 ozs. of tomato juice

2 cans of asparagus (14½ oz.), cut up, including liquid
14 ozs. water
2 tbsps. dried onion flakes
½ tsp. of salt
⅛ tsp. of oregano
Several sprinkles of pepper
¼ tsp. of garlic powder
1½ envelopes of Sweet 'N Low

In a blender, combine asparagus, asparagus liquid and onion flakes and blend until smooth. Place in a saucepan and add all of the other ingredients except the sweetener; then, simmer for two to three minutes. Add the sweetener.

You may also serve this with bean sprouts!

This soup can stay in the refrigerator for several days. If you prefer, you can also freeze it in small portions.

The recipe will serve four to six.

SPEEDY SAUERKRAUT SOUP

1 qt.-14-oz. can of tomato juice
1 lb.-11-oz. can of sauerkraut and liquid
2 cans of water (use empty sauerkraut can)
2 to 3 envelopes MBT Beef or Chicken Broth
Sweetener to taste (this takes quite a bit)

Cook all of the above ingredients, except the sweetener, in an uncovered pan at a slow simmer for about 1 to 1½ hours. Add sweetener to taste.

This can stay in the refrigerator for days and also freezes very well. It's a delicious, hearty soup.

This recipe will serve six to eight.

SPEEDY CREAM OF MUSHROOM SOUP

4-oz. can of mushrooms, including liquid
6 ozs. of water
2 to 3 tbsps. of powdered nonfat dry milk
Salt and pepper to taste
Dried onion flakes (optional)

Mix all of the above ingredients in a blender. Heat thoroughly and serve. This recipe will serve two.

CREAM OF CHICKEN SOUP

1½ envelopes MBT Chicken Broth
10 ozs. of boiling water
2 tsps. dried onion flakes
2 ozs. of parsnip, peeled and diced
2 sprigs of dill, or ⅛ tsp. dill weed
1 to 2 tbsps. powdered skimmed milk

Bring broth, water, onion flakes, parsnip and dill to a boil. Simmer, covered, for about 7 to 10 minutes, until parsnip is soft. If using fresh dill, remove from pot. Place the ingredients in a blender and add powdered skimmed milk. Whirl until smooth. Reheat.

This contains 2 ozs. of limited vegetable and 2 tbsps. of powdered milk. Count these toward your daily allowance. Use this at your dinner meal only.

CREAM OF MUSHROOM SOUP

½ lb. of fresh mushrooms
2 cups of water
⅓ cup of powdered milk

2 envelopes MBT Chicken or Vegetable Broth
1 tbsp. dried onion flakes
½ tsp. salt
Sprinkles of pepper
Sprinkles of garlic powder
½ tsp. freeze-dried chives

Clean and slice mushrooms. Cook all of the above ingredients for a few minutes until the mushrooms are soft. Serves 4.

Remember to count the milk in your daily allotment.

CREAM OF PEA SOUP

4 ozs. canned peas
½ cup of liquified skimmed milk
Salt and pepper to taste

Place above in a blender for five to ten seconds. Heat slowly.

Variation: 1) Add ½ can of mushrooms, drained; 2) Add 1 tsp. dried onion flakes before blending.

This is a limited dinner vegetable—4-oz. serving. Remember to count the milk toward your daily allowance.

TOMATO-VEGETABLE BOUILLON

12 ozs. tomato juice
1 envelope MBT Vegetable Broth
1 tbsp. chives
Salt and pepper
Pinch sweet basil

¼ tsp. dried parsley flakes
Sweetener to taste

Bring all of the above ingredients to a boil. This recipe will serve 2.

Count the tomato juice as part of your daily allotment.

CREAM OF TOMATO SOUP

1 46-oz. can of tomato juice
1 cup nonfat dry milk
1 tsp. salt
1 bay leaf
2 tsps. of vinegar
2 tbsps. dried onion flakes
1 envelope Sweet 'N Low
2 cloves
½ tsp. parsley
½ tsp. basil
1 rib celery and leaves, cut up

Cook above ingredients (low simmer) for about five minutes. Strain. Serve hot or cold.

FISH SOUP

2 ozs. leftover fish, cooked
½ cup tomato juice
1 tsp. dried vegetable flakes
Pinch of sweet basil
Pinch of garlic powder
Salt and pepper to taste

ash of Sauté Onion Powder
cup liquified skimmed milk

Flake fish and add all remaining ingredients except
he milk. Bring to a boil in a sauce pan. Scald the ½ cup
f milk and add to fish mixture. Serve at once! (This
hould not be reheated!)

Count the fish and milk toward your daily
llowance.

NOTE: You can use 2 ozs. of any other fish for lunch
vith a cold dressing (pp. 142-146). For dinner, you can
erve 4 ozs. of fish to make up fish allowance for meal.

1ANHATTAN CLAM CHOWDER

(8 ozs.) bottle of clam juice
cans minced clams, including liquid (drained clams
to weigh 8 ozs.)
cup Sacramento Tomato Juice
tbsps. dehydrated vegetable flakes
tbsp. dried onion flakes
½ to 1 envelope of Sweet 'N Low
everal good pinches of thyme leaves

Drain liquid from the clams into a saucepan and add
lam juice, tomato juice, vegetable and onion flakes
nd thyme leaves. Simmer, uncovered, for about five
ninutes, until dried vegetables are reconstituted and
ender. Add the clams and sweetener, and turn the heat
ff.

Use this as a luncheon meal, or first course, for
wo—followed by a shellfish main course of 4-oz. por-
ions. You can also serve this as a dinner meal by using

6 ozs. of minced clams. The rest of the recipe remains the same.

NOTE: A 10-oz. can of minced clams weighs 4 to 5 ozs. when drained.

QUICK ONION BOUILLON

1 envelope MBT Beef Broth
1 cup water
1 tbsp. onion flakes, crumbled

Cook all of above for a few minutes. Serve with ONE sprinkle of Parmesan cheese!

This is unlimited!

TUNA OR CLAM CHOWDER

10 ozs. Clamato Juice
1 tbsp. dried onion flakes
1 tbsp. dried vegetable flakes
¼ tsp. thyme
6 ozs. tuna fish or clams, drained
½ cup french-cut string beans, cooked and drained (optional)
1 small, or ½ of a large, green Italian frying pepper, diced
4 ozs. of cooked, drained, peas
Several pinches of sweetener (or up to ½ envelope of Sweet 'N Low)

Bring Clamato Juice to a boil. Add onion flakes, vegetable flakes, thyme and green pepper; then, lower the flame to a simmer. Cook for 3 to 4 minutes, uncovered, to soften vegetables. Then add the tuna fish

(or clams), string beans (optional), peas and sweetener.
Bring to a boil.

This is a good, filling dinner meal. If it is to be used
for lunch, leave out the peas and reduce the fish to 4
ozs. and Clamato Juice to 8 ozs. Use french-cut string
beans if using recipe for lunch.

This is a special favorite of mine with tuna!

COLD TOMATO BISQUE #1

46-oz. can of tomato juice
2/3 cup of nonfat dry milk
2 tbsps. lemon juice
3 tsps. Worcestershire Sauce
½ tsp. tabasco
1½ to 2 tsps. salt (or more, to taste)
Several shakes of freshly ground pepper

Combine all of the ingredients and chill. Serve cold
or "on the rocks." This recipe will serve 4 to 6.

COLD TOMATO BISQUE #2

2 cups of tomato juice
2 cups of buttermilk
6 drops of tabasco
2 tsps. lemon juice or ReaLemon
1 tsp. of Worcestershire Sauce
¾ tsp. of salt
Several shakes of freshly ground pepper
Pinch of sweetener

Combine all ingredients and check seasonings. Serve

well chilled. You may wish to add freeze-dried chives when serving.

This will stay well in the refrigerator for several days. This recipe serves 3 to 4.

OYSTER STEW

1 8-oz. can of oysters, including liquid
2 ozs. of water
2 ozs. of evaporated skimmed milk
4 ozs. of liquified skimmed milk
1 tbsp. dried onion flakes
¼ to ½ tsp. of salt
½ envelope MBT Chicken Broth (dry)
Sprinkles of pepper and paprika
1 tbsp. fresh chives, or 1 tsp. freeze-dried chives
1 tbsp. fresh parsley, or 1 tsp. dried parsley flakes
Several drops of butter extract (optional)
Several drops of Worcestershire Sauce (optional)

Cook onion flakes in 2 ozs. of water for a minute or two to soften. Add all of the other ingredients except the oysters and bring to a boil. Add oysters and reheat to just under the boiling point.

Remember to count the milk toward your daily allowance.

This recipe serves one for lunch; two for a first course if you follow it with 2 ozs. of Shellfish for lunch or 4 ozs. of Shellfish for dinner.

NOTE: Drained measurement of oysters is 5 ozs. Therefore, remove 1 oz. of oysters **before** starting this dish.

CRAB BISQUE

1 cup of tomato juice
1 cup of water
1 tbsp. Durkee's Instant Chopped Onion
2 tbsps. of dehydrated vegetable flakes
½ cup of diced celery
¼ tsp. of thyme leaves
¼ to ½ tsp. of salt
Several sprinkles of pepper
4 ozs. of crabmeat, frozen or canned
⅓ cup dry skimmed milk, or 2 ozs. of evaporated
   skimmed milk
4 ozs. of water, if using the dry skimmed milk

Place one cup of tomato juice and one cup of water
in a saucepan with onion, vegetable flakes, celery and
thyme leaves. Cook, uncovered, until the vegetables
are softened and the liquid has thickened. Add the
crabmeat, salt and pepper, and allow to stand for a few
minutes. Then, mix the powdered milk with 4 ozs. of
water, and add to the mixture. Reheat to serve (do not
boil).

If you are using this for lunch, make Crab Cocktail
with the other 2 ozs. of crabmeat needed to complete
your luncheon, adding Seafood Cocktail Sauce (p.
147).

If Crab Bisque is being used for an evening meal,
make a Chef's Salad (pp. 137-138), using 4 ozs. of
crabmeat for protein. Serves 2 for lunch or dinner!

GAZPACHO SOUP

1 qt. of tomato juice
1½ cucumbers, peeled and cut up
1 clove of garlic, cut up
1 green pepper, cut up
2 tbsps. of dried onion flakes
1 tbsp. of white vinegar
1 tsp. of salt (more, if desired)
Several shakes of pepper
2 to 3 dashes of red pepper sauce
½ envelope of Sweet 'N Low

Blend garlic, ½ of the green pepper, onion flakes and
1 cut-up cucumber until smooth. Add to the othe
ingredients and chill. Serve well chilled. Pass extr
diced cucumber and diced green pepper when servin
Serves 6 to 8.

NOTE: Tomato juice is to be computed in your dai
allowance.

SISTER ANNE'S COLD SHAV (or Spinach Soup

1 lb. fresh shav (sourgrass) or spinach
1 qt. plus 1 cup water
2 small pieces of sour salt
2 tsps. of salt
Dash of sweetener

Remove stems from the shav and wash well (it's sar
dy); drain. Cut the shav by holding in your hand ar
cutting off one inch lengths.

Bring water to a boil and add two small pieces
sour salt. Add cut-up shav to the boiling water. Brir

ack to boil and cook on medium heat for three
minutes. Turn off heat and allow to cool in pan. Chill
several hours. Add 2 tsps. or more of salt, to taste. Add
sweetener. Serve cold with 2 tbsps. of buttermilk and
cut-up cucumber.

This is ⅛ of your daily milk allowance.

SPEEDY BORSCHT

-oz. can julienne cut beets and liquid
  (2 ozs. beets plus 2 ozs. liquid)
small piece of sour salt
  (size of a very small pea)
Dash of salt
½ envelope of Sweet 'N Low
ozs. water
ozs. buttermilk

Bring water, sour salt, salt, beets and liquid to a boil,
and simmer for a few minutes. Cool and refrigerate.

Serve with sliced cucumbers and two tbsps. of
buttermilk.

This is a limited vegetable. A dinner serving is 4 ozs.
Buttermilk is to be computed in your daily allowance.

COLD SPINACH SOUP #1

pkgs. of frozen chopped spinach
small pieces of sour salt
½ quarts of water
tbsp. plus 2 tsps. of salt, or to taste
buttermilk (2 tbsps. to a cup)

Cook chopped spinach, water and sour salt, uncovered, for ten minutes. Allow to cool. Add salt to taste. For each 8-oz. serving, add 2 tbsps. of buttermilk. You may wish to serve this with sliced cucumbers.

Soup is unlimited. Buttermilk is to be counted toward your daily milk allowance.

COLD SPINACH SOUP #2

1 pkg. frozen chopped spinach
1 qt. of water
3 to 4 pieces of sour salt
Salt and pepper to taste
1 onion—to be removed whole after a few minutes of cooking (optional)
Buttermilk

Bring all of the above ingredients, except the buttermilk, to a boil, and simmer 5 to 8 minutes. Remove onion and allow the soup to cool. Refrigerate. Serve with 2 tbsps. of buttermilk and sliced cucumbers for each serving.

Meats

Please note that this section is devoted more to veal than to beef or lamb. Since we are limited to eating beef or lamb three times weekly, what better choice than a broiled steak or a roast leg of lamb which are so simple to prepare!

The **challenge** is cooking veal to simulate a beef meal . . . **that's** the difficult thing!

Try Veal Stuffed Peppers, Veal Stuffed Cabbage, Veal Chili, Sloppy Joe . . . or any of the Veal Loaf recipes in this section. Really delectable!

ROAST BEEF

Roast Beef, Prime Ribs of Beef, Sirloin Roast, or other
   (With bone, or boned and rolled)
Salt, pepper, garlic powder and Ehler's Sauté Onion
   Powder, to taste

Sprinkle seasonings liberally on top, bottom and sides of roast and allow to remain in refrigerator for 1 to 2 hours or more before cooking. Preheat oven to 325° and place meat thermometer in center of roast. (Do not place the thermometer near the bones!) Place

45

the roast on a rack in the roasting pan and roast, uncovered, until the thermometer reads:

140° F.—Rare
160° F.—Medium
170° F.—Well done

Serve 4-oz. portions for lunch; 6-oz. portions for
dinner!

BROILED FLANK STEAK

Well-trimmed flank steak
Mustard
"Legal" Chili Sauce (p. 151)

Spread a layer of mustard on a well-trimmed, scored
flank steak. Then spread a layer of Chili Sauce on top
of the mustard. Allow to marinate for an hour or two in
the refrigerator. Broil four inches away from the heating element for 4 to 7 minutes. Remove the steak from
the broiler and turn it over. Make a thin layer of mustard and then a layer of Chili Sauce on top of the steak.
Broil 4 to 7 minutes longer. Slice thin, against the grain.

If you are serving many people and more than one
flank steak is to be used, place them on a rack in a
400° pre-heated oven and bake for 15 to 25 minutes,
uncovered. Cook according to family's preference.

Serve 4-oz. portions for lunch; 6-oz. portions for
dinner.

Try this on your outdoor grill. Superb!

BAKED FRANKFURTERS WITH SAUER-KRAUT

8 ozs. of all-beef frankfurters

1 medium-sized can of sauerkraut
½ to 1 tbsp. of caraway seeds

Make slashes along the ends and sides of the frankfurters and broil for a few minutes. Cut into 2" pieces. Combine sauerkraut, caraway seeds and frankfurters. Bake, uncovered, at 350° for about 20 to 30 minutes.

SUKIYAKI

16 ozs. of sirloin steak, filet mignon tidbits
    or frozen steaks for sandwiches (cut ¼"
    thick by 1½" long)
1 4-oz. onion, sliced thin in rings
5 stalks of celery, cut diagonally
8 to 10 large mushrooms, sliced
1 lb. fresh spinach leaves, cut in half
4 ozs. of pea pods and bamboo shoots, combined
4 tbsps. KikkoMan Soy Sauce
2 envelopes Sweet 'N Low
2 to 3 ozs. of water

In an uncovered Teflon skillet, stew the celery, onions and mushrooms in a little water for about five minutes on a fairly high flame. Add the soy sauce and sweetener and stir. Then, add the steak strips, spinach leaves and pea pods and bamboo shoots, and cook 5 to 8 minutes longer.

This recipe will serve 2 for dinner.

NOTE: If you like more of a beef flavor, add ½ envelope of MBT Beef Broth. Onions, pea pods and bamboo shoots are limited vegetables.

Beef slices thin best when it is slightly frozen.

FRANKFURTER-VEGETABLE CASSEROLE

8 ozs. of tomato juice
½ green pepper, diced fine
1 tbsp. dried onion flakes
1 tsp. prepared mustard
½ tsp. Worcestershire Sauce
⅛ tsp. garlic powder
1 oz. of wine vinegar
¼ tsp. of salt
Several sprinkles of pepper
½ envelope of Sweet 'N Low
8 ozs. of all-beef frankfurters
4 ozs. of cooked peas and carrots
½ package of french-cut string beans, cooked

Make barbecue sauce by cooking tomato juice, green pepper, onion flakes, mustard, Worcestershire Sauce, garlic powder, wine vinegar, salt and pepper, in an uncovered saucepan for about ½ hour. Add sweetener.

Broil frankfurters; then, slice in 1″ pieces. Arrange vegetables in a low casserole. Place the sliced frankfurters on top of the vegetables. Pour the barbecue sauce over the frankfurters and bake, uncovered, in 400° oven for about 30 minutes.

This recipe will serve 1 for dinner.

ROAST LEG OF LAMB

3 to 4 lb. leg of lamb
Salt
Pepper

3 to 4 garlic cloves, cut into pieces
1 tsp. of dried rosemary or thyme

Preheat the oven to 325° F. Gash the surface of the roast and insert small pieces of garlic. Sprinkle the meat with salt and pepper; then, pat the rosemary or thyme over the entire roast.

Place the roast in a low, uncovered, pan (do not add any water) and cook for 2 to 2¼ hours.

If you are using a meat thermometer, the roast will be medium done at 175° F.; well done at 180° F.

It is not necessary to turn the roast over to baste.

Serve 4-oz. portions for lunch; 6-oz. portions for dinner.

LAMB OR BEEF KEBABS

Marinade
1 cup of wine vinegar
1 cup of water
3 bay leaves
½ tsp. of oregano leaves, crushed, or ½ tsp. of thyme
    leaves
1 tsp. of salt
⅛ tsp. of pepper
2 tbsps. dried onion flakes
2 cloves of garlic, split,
    or ½ tsp. of garlic powder
1 tsp. of prepared mustard
1 envelope of Sweet 'N Low

Simmer all of the above ingredients, except the sweetener, for 3 to 5 minutes, in an uncovered

saucepan. Allow to cool, then remove the bay leaves
and add the sweetener.

Kebabs
2 lbs. sirloin steak, London broil
  or lamb cubes
1 lb. of medium-sized mushrooms,
  or whole canned mushrooms
Cherry tomatoes or quartered tomatoes
4 green peppers, cut into chunks
1 fresh pineapple, cut into chunks
1 can of whole onions, drained

Cut meat into cubes, and pour the marinade over the
meat. Cover and refrigerate for eight hours or longer.
When ready to use, drain and reserve the marinade.
Alternate the meat, vegetables and pineapple cubes on
skewers. Cook over charcoal. You can also make this
indoors by using the broiler for 15 to 20 minutes. Baste
with the marinade and turn the skewers often.
Serves 4 for dinner or 7 for lunch.
If you are using this recipe for lunch, do not use
tomatoes or onions as they are limited to dinner use.
Count the pineapple toward your daily fruit allowance
(¼ of a pineapple equals one fruit).

BONELESS VEAL ROAST

4-lb. veal roast, boned and rolled
Salt, pepper, garlic powder, oregano and
  paprika, to taste
2 tbsps. dried onion flakes
3 ozs. of water

Ehler's Sauté Onion Powder, to taste
1 bay leaf (optional)

Season veal very heavily with salt, pepper, oregano, garlic powder (be generous with this), paprika, and the onion powder. Place the onion flakes, bay leaf and water in the bottom of a roasting pan and sprinkle with paprika. Place the roast in the pan and cover. Bake in a 350° oven for 1½ hours; then, uncover the roast and turn it over. Raise the heat to 375° and bake for 20 minutes, or until the meat is fork tender.

Serve 4-oz. portions for lunch; 6-oz. portions for dinner!

This will freeze extremely well. It also makes a very good cold sandwich at lunch!

VEAL CHILI

1 lb. raw ground veal
1 clove of garlic, diced, or
  ¼ tsp. of garlic powder
Sprinkles of black pepper
½ tsp. of salt, or more (to taste)
1 tsp. of chili powder
½ envelope of Sweet 'N Low
2 tbsps. dried onion flakes
12 ozs. of tomato juice
½ tsp. paprika (optional)

Brown the veal in a Teflon pan, stirring to break up the meat into little pieces. Add all of the spices and mix through the meat. Pour on the tomato juice and simmer, uncovered, until all of the liquid has cooked down . . . 15 to 25 minutes.

This will serve two for dinner.

This freezes very well.

Variation: Add ½ of a green pepper, diced, to the mixture while adding the spices.

SLOPPY JOE

1 lb. ground veal
1½ cups of tomato juice
1 tsp. salt
¼ tsp. each of garlic powder, thyme,
    oregano, turmeric and sweet basil
1 envelope of Sweet 'N Low
1½ tbsps. dried onion flakes
Sprinkles of pepper

Brown the meat in a Teflon skillet. Add all of the seasonings except the sweetener; then, pour the tomato juice over all. Cook, uncovered, until **all** of the liquid has cooked down . . . about 12 to 15 minutes. Add the sweetener and serve.

You may serve 4-oz. portions for lunch; 6-oz. portions for dinner.

This is as luscious as any Sloppy Joe, and it freezes well, too.

VEAL BALLS WITH CABBAGE

Veal Mixture
2 lbs. ground veal
1 tsp. Lawry's Seasoned Salt
½ tsp. garlic powder
⅛ tsp. black pepper
1 tsp. parsley flakes

¼ tsp. oregano
½ cup of tomato juice
2 tbsps. dried onion flakes
1 envelope MBT Chicken Broth

Soup
1 large head of cabbage
1 red pepper
1 green pepper (or 2 green peppers if
    the red pepper is not available)
3 large stalks of celery, cut up
1½ tbsps. of onion flakes
4 cups of Sacramento Tomato Juice
Lemon juice, to taste
Salt, pepper and sweetener, to taste

Mix the veal mixture ingredients together and shape into balls. (Have your hands wet for easier handling of the meat.) Brown the balls in a Teflon pan.

While browning the veal balls, set 4 cups of tomato juice to cook. Cut up the cabbage into chunks, slice the peppers and celery, and add to the tomato juice while it's cooking. Also, add the onion flakes, about ½ cup of lemon juice, about ½ tsp. of salt, and a sprinkling of pepper. When the soup is cooking, add the browned veal balls to the pot and cook, with the cover half on the pot, for about two hours. Add sweetener to taste.

Remember to count the tomato juice as part of your daily allowance.

Serve 2-oz. portions as an appetizer; 4-oz. portions for lunch; 6-oz. portions for dinner. Only the veal is to be weighed!

Variation: Instead of cabbage and the tomato juice, use 3 to 4 envelopes of MBT Chicken Broth, 3 cups of water (part mushroom liquid), 1 large can of mushrooms, and ¼ tsp. of oregano. Then follow the above recipe.

This freezes very well and will stay in the refrigerator for several days.

VEAL LOAF #1

8 ozs. ground veal
4 ozs. of Sacramento Tomato Juice
1 tbsp. Worcestershire Sauce
Pinch of garlic powder
M.S.G. (optional)
½ tsp. of salt
Sprinkle of pepper
1 tbsp. dried onion flakes
2 ozs. of canned mushrooms, drained

Mix all of the ingredients together and allow to stand until the tomato juice is absorbed. Bake at 350° for 1 hour, or until well browned.

Serves 1.

VEAL LOAF #2

2 lbs. raw ground veal
1 tsp. of Lawry's Seasoned Salt
1 tsp. of garlic powder
⅛ tsp. of black pepper
½ tsp. of dried parsley flakes, or
    1 tbsp. of freshly chopped parsley

¼ tsp. of oregano
2 tbsps. of onion flakes
½ cup of Sacramento Tomato Juice
4 oz. can of mushrooms, drained (optional)

Combine all of the above ingredients and form into a loaf, or, you can use the small Teflon loaf pan (7⅜″ x 3⅝″ x 2¼″) which is my preference. Bake, uncovered, at 350° for 1 hour and 10 to 15 minutes.

Serve a 4-oz. portion for lunch; a 6-oz. portion for dinner.

Remember to count the tomato juice toward your daily allowance.

This freezes well and can also be used cold in a "sandwich" (p. 12) for lunch!

VEAL STUFFED PEPPERS

3 lbs. ground veal
8 green peppers
6 ozs. plus 8 ozs. tomato juice
3 tbsps. dried onion flakes
3 tbsps. of dried vegetable flakes
1 tbsp. of salt
¼ tsp. of pepper
¼ tsp. of garlic powder, or more
1 tbsp. Worcestershire Sauce

Cut the peppers in half. Mix the meat with all of the other ingredients except the final 8 ozs. of tomato juice. Weigh off 4-oz. portions of the meat, and then stuff the peppers. Any meat left over can be used in a Veal Loaf. Place the peppers in a casserole dish and pour 8 ozs. of tomato juice around the peppers. Bake, covered, for 1

hour, at 375°. Uncover the pan and baste the peppers.
Return the pan to the oven for another ½ hour. Baste
several times.

You may serve two for dinner. If you plan to use this
recipe for lunch, weigh off 3-oz. portions before stuffing and serve two.

NOTE: Large quantities are suggested here since this
is time-consuming to make and freezes extremely well.
Also, your entire family will undoubtedly enjoy this
very much!

VEAL BALLS STROGANOFF

Veal Mixture
1½ lbs. ground veal
1½ tbsps. of dried onion flakes
1 tsp. of salt
⅛ tsp. of pepper
¼ tsp. of garlic powder
½ envelope of MBT Chicken Broth
3 ozs. of water
1 tsp. of parsley flakes

Sauce Mixture
1 cup chicken bouillon
1½ tsps. of dried onion flakes
1½ tsps. Worcestershire Sauce
¾ tsp. of powdered mustard
½ cup of buttermilk
4-oz. can of sliced mushrooms
   (you can use the mushroom liquid
   to help make up the bouillon)

Mix the meat mixture ingredients and form into

small balls. Brown quickly in a Teflon skillet. After the veal balls are browned, remove them from the pan. Add all of the sauce mixture ingredients, except the buttermilk, to the skillet and bring to a boil. Return the veal balls to the skillet and allow to simmer for about 15 to 20 minutes, uncovered. If the sauce cooks down during this time, add boiling water to the pan. When the veal balls are thoroughly cooked and the sauce is reduced and thick, turn off the heat. Add the buttermilk and serve immediately. This freezes very well.

Serve 4-oz. portions for lunch; 6-oz. portions for dinner.

VEAL LOAF—ITALIAN STYLE

1 lb. raw ground veal
1½ tbsps. dried onion flakes
4-oz. can of mushrooms, including the liquid
¼ tsp. of fennel seeds, or more
1 garlic clove, or ¼ tsp. of garlic powder
Salt and pepper to taste
1 envelope MBT Beef Broth
4 drops Worchestershire Sauce, or more

Mix all of the above ingredients together and place in a small Teflon loaf pan. Bake at 350° for 1¼ hours.

This will serve two for dinner.

Variation: Form the meat into patties and grill out-doors.

VEAL PIE

Crust
4 slices of white bread, baked at 250°

for about 20 to 30 minutes
2 tbsps. nonfat dry milk
½ envelope of Sweet 'N Low
2 tbsps. of water

Filling
1½ lbs. ground veal
1½ tsp. of salt
Several good pinches of pepper
⅛ tsp. of garlic powder
1½ tbsps. dried onion flakes
3 ozs. of cooked-down tomato juice
   (start with 6 ozs.)

Blend bread into crumbs. Add the dry milk and the sweetener. Mix the water through the mixture and press the moist crumbs into the bottom of a Teflon pie plate. Combine all of the filling ingredients and form into a flat circle (use a soup plate). Gently place on top of bread crust, and bake, uncovered, at 325° for about 1 hour.

This recipe is to be served at lunch only, and is ample for four.

DILL PICKLE VEAL LOAF

1 lb. raw ground veal
6 tbsps. kosher pickle, finely diced
1½ tbsps. dried onion flakes
1 tsp. salt
⅛ tsp. of pepper
4 ozs. of tomato juice, cooked down
¼ tsp. Worcestershire Sauce
⅛ tsp. of garlic powder

Mix all of the above ingredients together and pack lightly into a 7⅜" x 3⅝" x 2¼" Teflon loaf pan. Bake, uncovered, at 350° for an hour and 10 minutes. If there is too much liquid in the pan after about ¾ of an hour, pour a little **(not all)** off. (This freezes well.)

Serve 4-oz. portions for lunch; 6-oz. portions for dinner. This is very good served cold, too.

VEAL BALLS IN BARBECUE SAUCE

1 lb. raw ground veal
2 ozs. of water
1 tbsp. of dried onion flakes
1 tsp. of salt
Sprinkles of pepper
⅛ tsp. of garlic powder
½ tsp. of parsley flakes (optional)
1 cup of Barbecue Sauce #2 (p. 150)
1 cup of boiling water

Mix meat with 2 ozs. of water; then, add the onion flakes, salt, pepper, garlic powder and parsley flakes. Wet your hands and shape the meat into balls. Brown in a Teflon pan.

Mix the Barbecue Sauce #2 with boiling water and simmer for a minute in an uncovered saucepan. Drop the browned veal balls into the simmering sauce and continue to simmer, uncovered, for about ¾ to 1 hour, or until the sauce has thickened.

NOTE: This may be used for lunch in 4-oz portions or for dinner in 6-oz. portions. (It freezes well.)

Use this recipe for parties; nobody has to know it is dieter's food.

VEAL BALL STEW

1 lb. raw ground veal
2 ozs. of Sacramento Tomato Juice
1 tbsp. dried onion flakes
1 tsp. of salt
Sprinkles of black pepper
2 tbsps. of Italian parsley, cut fine
⅛ tsp. each of garlic powder
   and crushed rosemary
2 shakes of Parmesan cheese
1 envelope MBT Chicken Broth
8 ozs. of boiling water
4 ozs. of frozen peas and carrots, defrosted
4 ozs. of frozen string beans, defrosted

Mix the veal with the tomato juice, onion flakes, salt, pepper, Italian parsley, rosemary, garlic powder and Parmesan cheese. Shape the mixture into balls and brown in a Teflon skillet, uncovered. Add the broth and boiling water and simmer, uncovered, until liquid is reduced to about 3 ozs. . .about 15 minutes.

Add peas and carrots and the string beans. Simmer, covered, until the vegetables are tender (you may have to add more water). (This freezes well).

Count the tomato juice toward your daily allowance.

This will serve two for dinner only as the recipe includes a limited dinner vegetable.

ROLLED VEAL LOAF

Meat Mixture
1 lb. raw ground veal
½ envelope MBT Chicken Broth

1 tbsp. dried onion flakes
1 tsp. of salt
⅛ tsp. of pepper
¼ tsp. of garlic powder
4 ozs. of cooked-down tomato juice
⅛ tsp. of paprika

Stuffing Mixture
1 pkg. of frozen cauliflower
4 to 6 ozs. of water
½ envelope MBT Chicken Broth

Meat Mixture Directions

Mix all ingredients together and pat into an oblong shape on waxed paper. The loaf should be about 6″ x 8″ and almost ½″ thick.

Strffing Directions

Cook cauliflower, water and broth until vegetable is soft. Place cauliflower in a blender and add several tbsps. of cooking liquid. Blend until well mashed. Then place the cauliflower on top of the veal. Roll from narrow end, using waxed paper to help you roll . . . in jelly-roll fashion. When shaped properly, turn into a 7⅜″ x 3⅝″ x 2¼″ Teflon loaf pan. Remove the waxed paper. Bake at 350° for 1 hour and 10 minutes, or longer.

This will serve 2 for dinner!

VEAL RIBS

Breast of veal, cut into ribs
1 envelope MBT Chicken Broth
1 cup of water

2 tbsps. dried onion flakes
2 cloves of garlic, or ½ tsp. of garlic powder
Salt and pepper to taste
Paprika, spread liberally

Put the broth, water, onion flakes and seasonings in the bottom of a baking pan. Add the ribs, cover the pan, and bake at 350° for 1½ hours. Then, uncover the pan for ½ hour.

This is difficult to weigh. I suggest that you weigh off 10 ozs., including the bones. Re-weigh the bones after the meat has been eaten, and replace the meat weight to equal 6 ozs.

CHINESE VEAL RIBS

1 breast of veal, split like spare ribs
2 ozs. of orange juice
1 garlic clove, or ¼ tsp. of garlic powder
Soy sauce and sweetener, to taste

Marinate the ribs in the above ingredients overnight. Turn the ribs several times. Bake in the marinade, covered, for 1½ hours at 350°. Uncover the pan and bake ½ hour longer.

Count the orange juice as part of your daily fruit allowance.

NOTE: Weigh the veal and bones. Start with about 10-12 ozs.; then, re-weigh the bones after eating. Serve 4-oz. portions for lunch; 6-oz. portions for dinner!

VEAL CUTLET ITALIANO

1 lb. slice of veal cutlet (thick)

3 to 4 tbsps. of cooked-down tomato juice
1 tbsp. dried onion flakes
½ tsp. of Italian seasoning
Salt and pepper to taste
Pinch of sweetener

Simmer all of the above in a covered skillet until the meat is fork tender. Serves two for dinner!

Remember to count the tomato juice toward your daily allowance.

VEAL SCALLOPINI

1 lb. of veal, cut in thin slices
1 4-oz. can of mushrooms, including the liquid
1 envelope of MBT Beef Broth
⅛ tsp. of oregano
⅛ tsp. of garlic powder
Salt and pepper to taste
2 shakes of Parmesan cheese
4 to 5 ozs. of water

Brown the veal in a Teflon pan (add drops of water if the veal sticks). Measure the mushroom liquid with the water to make 8 ozs. of liquid. Add this to the veal with the broth, mushrooms, oregano, garlic powder, salt, pepper and cheese. Cook for a few minutes on a low flame until the meat is tender and the liquid has cooked down to a few ounces.

This recipe will serve two for dinner!

VEAL SAUSAGE PATTIE

3 ozs. of veal "sausage" pattie (p. 14)

Pan-fry the pattie in a Teflon skillet, uncovered, until the veal is well cooked and no longer pink. Serve with toast. The patties can be kept frozen until ready to be used.

This will serve one for breakfast; cook two patties for lunch.

VEAL PATTIES

1 lb. raw ground veal
1 tbsp. dried onion flakes
2 ozs. cooked-down tomato juice
½ green pepper, finely diced
⅛ tsp. garlic powder
½ tsp. salt
Sprinkle of pepper
Sprinkle of paprika
1 envelope MBT Chicken Broth, dry

Mix all of the above ingredients together and shape into patties. Broil or pan-broil (Teflon skillet) until the meat is well cooked. Serves two for dinner.

Count the tomato juice as part of your daily allowance.

NOTE: The patties can be frozen for future use.

BREAKFAST VEAL SAUSAGE

3 ozs. breakfast veal "sausage" (p. 14)

Slit the sausage in half the long way and pan fry cut side down until it is well done. Turn the meat over and fry until the casing loosens. Remove casing and continue cooking until "sausage" is brown and no longer pink. Serve with toast.

Serve 3 ozs. raw (2 ozs. cooked) for breakfast; 6 ozs. raw (4 ozs. cooked) for lunch! The meat can be kept in the freezer until it is needed.

VEAL PATTIES IN BARBECUE SAUCE

8 ozs raw ground veal
Barbecue Sauce #1 or #2 (pp. 149-150)
½ tsp. dried onion flakes
Several sprinkles of garlic powder

Mix the veal with the onion flakes, garlic powder and 2 tbsps. of Barbecue Sauce. Form into patties. Spoon several more tbsps. of Barbecue Sauce over the patties and broil until the veal is no longer pink.

This will serve one for dinner.

Remember to count the tomato juice in the Barbecue Sauce toward your daily allowance.

SPICY VEAL SAUSAGE CASSEROLE

8 ozs. of fresh veal "sausage" (p.14)
1 cup tomato juice
½ green pepper, diced
½ red pepper, diced (if available)
2 tbsps. of dehydrated vegetable flakes
1 tbsp. dried onion flakes

Slice the "sausage" in half the long way and brown well in a Teflon pan. Remove the casing. Add all of the other ingredients and simmer, uncovered, until the sauce is thickened and the vegetables are tender. This is the answer to a Sausage-Lover's dream.

Count the tomato juice toward your daily
allowance.

VEAL SAUSAGE AND EGGPLANT

8 ozs. fresh veal "sausage," cut in half (p. 14)
8 ozs. of tomato juice
1 long green Italian frying pepper, diced
4 ozs. of eggplant, peeled and cubed
1 tbsp. dried onion flakes
⅛ tsp. of garlic powder
⅛ tsp. of oregano
Sweetener

Brown the meat on both sides in a Teflon skillet.
Remove the casing. Add the tomato juice, onion flakes,
green pepper, garlic and oregano and cook, uncovered,
for 10 minutes. Add the eggplant cubes and continue
cooking, uncovered, for 5 minutes . . . until the
eggplant is cooked but still firm. Add a few sprinkles of
sweetener.

This recipe will serve one for dinner.

NOTE: You can alter this recipe for lunch by using 6
ozs. of veal "sausage," substituting cooked french-cut
string beans for the eggplant.

Make larger quantities for company. It's marvelous!

VEAL SAUSAGE PIZZA

1 slice enriched white bread, toasted
4 ozs. smoked "sausage" (p. 14)
4 tbsps. of tomato juice, cooked down with oregano,
    garlic, salt, pepper and a dash of
    sweetener, all to taste

Slice the bread through the middle with a serrated knife to make two thin slices. Place the bread, toasted side down, on the broiler pan. Spoon 2 tbsps. of tomato juice (sauce) over each piece of bread. Slice the "sausage" in ¼" pieces (round) and place on top of the sauce. Broil until the sauce is bubbly and the veal is browned slightly. You may have to use a knife and fork to eat this, but it's delicious.

Remember to count the tomato juice toward your daily allowance.

NOTE: Since the veal is smoked (already cooked), use actual weight for "after cooking" weight.

VEAL AND EGGPLANT STEW

1 eggplant, peeled and cut into cubes
1 onion, diced
2 garlic cloves
1 green pepper, diced
4-oz. can of mushrooms
16 ozs. of veal cubes
1 cup of tomato juice
Salt and pepper to taste
¼ to ½ tsp. of thyme or turmeric

Stew onion and garlic in a little water in a Teflon pan. Add the veal cubes and brown. Add the pepper and tomato juice and simmer for 20 minutes. Then, add the remaining ingredients and simmer for ½ hour longer, or until the meat is tender. If this gets too thick, add extra tomato juice or a little water.

This will serve two for dinner!

VEAL-ARTICHOKE STEW

1 lb. veal, cut up in cubes
8 ozs. of water
1 envelope MBT Chicken Broth
1 clove of garlic, or ¼ tsp. of garlic powder
1 tbsp. of dried onion flakes
1 cup of tomato juice
¼ tsp. of thyme, crushed
1 tsp. of salt
½ to 1 envelope of Sweet 'N Low
Several pinches of pepper
Several pinches of tarragon (optional)
1 package of frozen artichoke hearts

Simmer all of the ingredients, except the artichokes, in a covered saucepan for about 1 hour, or until the meat is tender. Add boiling water if the sauce cooks down too much. Add the frozen artichoke hearts and cook, covered, for 5 to 7 minutes. Check the seasoning as it may need more salt. Serves two for dinner!

You can freeze this dish for future use.

CHOPPED LIVER

3 lbs. beef liver, cut in pieces
    (or, you can use chicken liver)
4 to 6 tbsps. dried onion flakes
2 to 3 cups of water
3 envelopes MBT Chicken Broth
Garlic powder, salt and pepper, to taste

Cook the liver in water, onion flakes, seasonings and broth in an uncovered pot until the liver is no longer pink. Put the liver and drained onion flakes through a grinder. Add the liquid in which the liver was cooked, starting with ½ cup, until the mixture is the right consistency. Add several **additional** tbsps. of uncooked onion flakes (optional) and refrigerate. Before serving, correct the seasonings.

If desired, garnish with the white part of a hard-cooked egg.

Serve 4 ozs. for lunch; 6 ozs. for dinner.

NOTE: This recipe can be cut in half for smaller quantity. This takes time to make, however, and does freeze well.

LIVER, ONIONS, AND MUSHROOMS

8 ozs. beef liver, sliced thin,
    (or chicken livers, cut in half)
4 ozs. of fresh, diced onions
¼ lb. of sliced fresh mushrooms, or
    1 4-oz. can of sliced mushrooms
1 envelope MBT Chicken Broth
4 ozs. of water
Salt, pepper, garlic powder and
    paprika, to taste

Simmer the onions in water and broth in an uncovered skillet. Season with salt, pepper, garlic powder and paprika. If using fresh mushrooms, add them at this time and cook for a few minutes. Add the liver to the skillet (and, if using them, the canned mushrooms) and fry until the liver is slightly pink in the center.

This recipe will serve one for dinner.

NOTE: Onions are a limited vegetable for dinner only. If you are using liver for lunch, use 1 tbsp. of

onion flakes and 6 ozs. of liver. If you are using canned
mushrooms, use drained liquid in place of water.

CHICKEN LIVERS AND VEGETABLES IN FOIL

8 ozs. chicken livers (in half-frozen state)
½ green pepper, cut into strips
2 ozs. diced fresh onion
2 ozs. of diced carrots
1 to 2 ozs. of diced celery (optional)
1 envelope MBT Chicken Broth, dry
Several sprinkles of pepper
Several sprinkles of garlic powder

Make a packet out of a double thickness of
aluminum foil. Place 2 tbsps. of water in the bottom of
the foil packet. Place the livers in the packet, season
with garlic powder and pepper, add the vegetables, and
sprinkle the broth over all. Fold the packet with a
"drugstore" wrap.

Cook on your outdoor grill, or indoors, turning the
packet at least once.

This will serve 1 for dinner.

Poultry

Poultry is a great choice for the entire family . . . and it can be used for party dishes as well!

Chicken may be purchased whole or cut up into parts, whichever you prefer.

Roast chicken for your family; with leftovers (if you have any!), make Elegant Chicken à La King. Leftover chicken or turkey can be used to make Chicken Salad (pp. 138-139).

Freeze 4-oz. and 6-oz. portions of chicken and turkey, and use some of the recipes in this section.

Make Chicken Marengo, Curried Chicken with Beet Sauce, or Chicken and Eggplant Casserole for your nicest dinner parties. Your guests will not believe they are eating "dieter's food"!

ROASTED CHICKEN

2-2½ to 3 lb. broiler-fryers, whole
Salt, pepper and garlic powder, to taste
Ehler's Sauté Onion Powder, to taste
Paprika (optional)

Season the chickens generously with salt, pepper, garlic powder and onion powder, and place in a roast-

71

ing pan. Do not add water to the pan. Bake, uncovered, at 325° for 1 hour. Turn chickens over, breast
side down, and season the backs. Continue roasting for
½ hour. Turn the chickens back, breast side up, and
raise the heat to 375° for 15 minutes. Sprinkle with
paprika, if desired, and bake for another 10 minutes.

Serve 4-oz. portions for lunch; 6-oz. portions for
dinner.

Save leftovers for Elegant Chicken à La King or cold
Chicken Salad (pp. 138-139). Leftover chicken can also
be delicious in a Chef's Salad (pp. 137-138). If you wish
you can freeze the leftovers for a later meal.

NOTE: You might enjoy my "Bread" Stuffing (pp.
154-155).

STUFFED CHICKEN BREASTS

Chicken
2 whole chicken breasts
Water to cover the chicken
2 tbsps. of dried onion flakes
2 tbsps. of dried vegetable flakes
2 stalks of celery, diced
1 envelope MBT Chicken Broth

Cover the chicken with water. Add onion flakes,
celery, vegetable flakes and broth. Simmer for about 30
minutes.

Stuffing
1 package frozen cauliflower
4 ozs. of water
1 envelope MBT Chicken Broth
2 ozs. of canned mushrooms, drained

1 tbsp. dried onion flakes
1 tbsp. chopped parsley
Sprinkles of garlic powder
Sprinkles of pepper
¼ to ½ tsp. of poultry seasoning
Paprika

Prepare the stuffing by cooking the cauliflower in ½ package of broth and 4 ozs. of water until cauliflower is soft, but not mushy. Remove from the liquid and chop or cut into small pieces. Add the mushrooms which have been diced, dried onion flakes, parsley, ½ envelope of broth, pepper, garlic powder and poultry seasoning.

Stuff the cavity of the chicken breasts and sprinkle the stuffing with paprika. Lay the breasts on their sides in a low casserole dish and spoon some of the soup mixture (in which the chicken was cooked) into the bottom of the dish and around the stuffed chicken breasts. . . including the onion, vegetable flakes and celery (about ½″ high in the pan). Sprinkle the top of the chicken breasts well with paprika and bake, uncovered, in 350° oven for 20 to 30 minutes, or until well browned. If more liquid is needed, add soup stock.

NOTE: This serves two for dinner but can be used for lunch if 4-oz. portions of chicken are served. The stuffing is unlimited!

ELEGANT CHICKEN À LA KING

4 ozs. of fresh mushrooms, sliced
1 small green pepper, diced
1 carrot and 1 parsnip (4 ozs. combined)

¾ cup MBT Chicken Broth plus several
   ozs. to cook mushrooms and peppers
½ to 1¾ tsps. of dried onion flakes
½ to 1¾ tsps. of dried vegetable flakes
¼ cup of evaporated skimmed milk
6 ozs. of cooked chicken
Salt and pepper to taste
Diced pimientos

Simmer mushrooms and green pepper in a little
broth for a few minutes. Cook chicken in water to
which you have added onion flakes, dried vegetable
flakes, salt, pepper, peeled parsnips and peeled carrots.
Allow to cool slightly.

Blend ¾ cup of broth and ¼ cup of evaporated
skimmed milk, 4 ozs. of parsnips and carrots until
smooth. Add sauce to the chicken, diced peppers and
mushrooms, which have been simmered in a little
broth, and red pimientos. Sprinkle salt and pepper to
taste. Serves 1 for dinner.

CHICKEN DIVAN

16 ozs. of evaporated skimmed milk
8 fresh mushrooms
2 envelopes MBT Chicken Broth
12 grated fresh mushrooms
2 bunches of broccoli
1 tsp. Worcestershire Sauce
Several good shakes of nutmeg
Salt, pepper and paprika, to taste
24 ozs. of cooked chicken
Sprinkle of Parmesan cheese (optional)

Place evaporated milk, 8 mushrooms and broth in a blender and blend until smooth. Grate 12 mushrooms on the slicing side of the grater. Add this to the blended mixture, along with the Worcestershire Sauce, nutmeg, salt and pepper (taste the sauce before salting). Cook up the broccoli and drain. Place the broccoli in a casserole dish, and sprinkle with Parmesan cheese (optional). Place cooked chicken on top of the broccoli. Spoon the sauce on top and sprinkle with paprika. Bake at 350°, uncovered, for about 15 minutes, or until well heated. This is a great way to use leftover chicken (or turkey). Serves 6.

Count the milk toward the daily allowance.

This stays well in the refrigerator for several days and also freezes well. For smaller quantities, cut the recipe in half.

CHICKEN CACCIATORA

1½ cups cooked-down tomato juice (p. 9)

8 chicken breasts, split

6 ozs. of onion, diced fine

4 ozs. of carrots, diced fine

¼ cup of green pepper, diced fine

½ lb. sliced mushrooms, or
    4-oz. can of sliced mushrooms, drained

1 oz. white wine vinegar with basil
    (Spice Islands brand)

½ envelope of Sweet 'N Low

1 tsp. of salt

⅛ tsp. of pepper

1 clove of garlic or ¼ tsp. of garlic powder

½ tsp. of crushed basil
¼ tsp. of crushed oregano

Broil the chicken, skin-side up, for 5 to 10 minutes. Make a sauce of all of the other ingredients except the mushrooms and sweetener. Add the chicken to the sauce and simmer in a covered pan or skillet for about ¾ hour. Add the mushrooms and continue to cook, uncovered, for 10 to 15 minutes. Add the Sweet 'N Low, and serve. Serves 3 for dinner. Each portion contains 3 ozs. of limited dinner vegetable.

If you wish, you can make this dish ahead of time; it freezes very well.

CHICKEN WITH BARBECUE SAUCE

2 chickens, cut up

Barbecue Sauce #1 (pp. 149-150)

Marinate the chicken for several hours, or overnight. Bake, uncovered, in a 350° oven for 1¼ hours, or until tender.

Use this for your dinner meal only. Remember to count the tomato juice and onion toward your daily allowance. (This is fantastic on the grill! Cook the chicken partway on foil on the grill. When it's almost ready, place the chicken directly on the grill. Beware!—If you cook this too close to the coals, it will burn because of the barbecue sauce.)

You can freeze the sauce separately, or, if you wish, you can freeze the entire dish.

Variation: Try Barbecue Sauce #2 (p. 150).

SESAME CHICKEN

1 chicken, cut up
Salt, pepper, garlic powder and paprika,
  to taste
1 tbsp. dried onion flakes
4 ozs. of boiling water
½ to ⅔ package MBT Chicken Broth
1 tsp. of **toasted** sesame seeds

Season the chicken with salt, pepper, garlic powder and paprika. Dissolve the broth in boiling water and add the onion flakes. Place the liquid mixture in a shallow casserole dish. Put the chicken parts in the dish and bake, covered, at 350° for an hour. Remove the cover and put the toasted sesame seeds on top of the chicken. Return the casserole to the oven, uncovered, and bake for about 30 minutes longer. Serves 2 for dinner.

NOTE: This can be used for lunch in 4-oz. portions. It also freezes very well.

CHICKEN MARENGO

2½ to 3 lb. chicken, cut up
1 clove of garlic, diced
1 tsp. of salt
1 envelope MBT Chicken Broth
4-oz. can of mushrooms, or
  ¼ lb. of fresh mushrooms
6 ozs. of water and mushroom liquid, combined
2 ozs. of onions, diced
6 ozs. of tomatoes, peeled and diced
¼ tsp. of thyme leaves, crushed

⅛ tsp. of marjoram leaves, crushed
⅛ tsp. of pepper
Lemon juice
1 tbsp. of snipped parsley or
   1 tsp. of parsley flakes

Broil the chicken parts for a few minutes. Place the chicken, broth, mushroom liquid and water, garlic, and diced onion in a heavy covered skillet, and season with salt, pepper, thyme and marjoram leaves. Simmer, covered, for 35 to 40 minutes. Add the peeled, diced tomatoes and the mushrooms and continue cooking for 5 minutes longer. Add the parsley and sprinkle lightly with the lemon juice, to taste. Check the seasonings . . . you may want to add more thyme. Serves 2.

NOTE: This includes 8 ozs. of a limited dinner vegetable. It's a wonderful party dish. Try it!

CHINESE CASSEROLE

6 ozs. cooked chicken or turkey
1 can chinese vegetables, drained
4 ozs. of bamboo shoots or cooked pea pods
½ package of cooked french-cut string beans
1 tbsp. of orange juice
4-oz. can of sliced mushrooms
1 tbsp., or more, of the mushroom liquid
1 envelope MBT Chicken Broth (do not add water)
4 to 7 capsful of KikkoMan Soy Sauce

Heat all of the above ingredients in a Teflon skillet, uncovered, Stir gently until well heated. The dish measurements, of course, are perfect for a dinner for 1.

This recipe contains a 4-oz. portion of limited

vegetables (bamboo shoots or peapods. My preference is a combination of both) and 1 tbsp. of orange juice.

ORIENTAL CHICKEN

3 chicken breasts, split
¼ cup, or more, of KikkoMan Soy Sauce
⅛ tsp. of garlic powder
1½ envelopes of Sweet 'N Low
⅛ tsp. of powdered ginger, or
   2 thin slices of ginger root
8 ozs. Cott's Orange Diet Soda

Sprinkle garlic powder on the chicken and marinate in the soy sauce, ginger and sweetener for several hours, turning the chicken frequently. Drain the marinade. Pour the soda over the chicken and bake, uncovered, for about 1½ hours in a 350° oven.

Serve a 4-oz. portion for lunch; a 6-oz. portion for dinner.

CHINESE CHICKEN AND VEGETABLES

4 ozs. of cooked, diced chicken
6 to 7 leaves of Chinese cabbage
4-oz. can of mushrooms in liquid
1 envelope of MBT Chicken Broth
½ can of bean sprouts (optional)
1 to 3 caps of KikkoMan Soy Sauce
1 envelope of Sweet 'N Low

Drain the liquid from the mushrooms and add water to this liquid to make 4 ozs. Bring it to a boil and add the broth, soy sauce, sweetener and chicken. Simmer for 1 minute; then, add all of the other ingredients and simmer for 1 minute longer.

This will serve 1 for lunch. To make this a dinner meal, use 6 ozs. of diced, cooked chicken or turkey, or shrimp as protein—and add 4 ozs. of bamboo shoots (or 2 ozs. of bamboo shoots and 2 ozs. of water chestnuts) which includes your limited dinner vegetable.

BAKED CREAMED CHICKEN

½ chicken, cut up
1 envelope MBT Chicken Broth
4 ozs. of boiling water
4 ozs. of evaporated skimmed milk
1 tbsp. of dried onion flakes
2 ozs. of **cooked** parsnip
  (or up to 4 ozs., if desired)
1½ tbsp. of fresh chives, cut up
1 clove of garlic, cut up
½ red or green pepper, diced
Salt and pepper to taste, if desired

Dissolve the broth in boiling water and allow to cool slightly. Add 4 ozs. of evaporated skimmed milk to the mixture and place in a blender. Add the onion flakes and the cooked parsnip and run the blender until you have the consistency of cream. Add the garlic and salt and pepper.

Place the chicken in a small, but heavy, baking dish. Pour the "cream" over the chicken, and top with the diced pepper and chives. Bake, covered, for 30 minutes in a pre-heated 350° oven. Uncover the chicken and continue baking for another ¾ hour, turning the chicken over several times. Serves 1 for dinner.

The parsnip is a limited dinner vegetable. If you are using 2 ozs. of parsnip, use 2 ozs. of any other limited dinner vegetable. If you are using 4 ozs. of parsnip, this is the amount of limited dinner vegetable allowed.

SPICY LIME CHICKEN

2 whole chicken breasts, split
3 tbsps. lime juice, or less to taste
⅛ tsp. of poultry seasoning
¼ tsp. of garlic powder
½ tsp. of salt
Sprinkles of pepper
¼ tsp. of thyme leaves, crushed
¼ to ½ tsp. of paprika
½ envelope of Sweet 'N Low

Broil the chicken, skin-side up, for 5 minutes. Remove chicken from the broiler and allow it to cool. Mix all of the other ingredients together and spread this mixture on the chicken. Allow to marinate in the refrigerator for 1 hour or longer.

Bake in a covered pan at 350°, skin-side up, for 30 to 40 minutes. Uncover the pan, turn the chicken over, raise the heat to 400° and add 2 ozs. or more of water to the pan juices. Bake for about 15 minutes longer. Turn the chicken skin-side up for at least the last 5 minutes of cooking time.

You may serve 4-oz. portions for lunch; 6-oz. portions for dinner.

CURRIED CHICKEN WITH BEET SAUCE

1½ chickens, cut up in eighths
4 ozs. freshly diced onion
3 tbsps. dried onion flakes
1 clove of garlic, minced
1 scant tsp. of curry powder
Salt and pepper to taste
3 tbsps. of cooked-down tomato juice
¼ tsp. of powdered ginger
1½ cups of water
1½ tbsps. of lemon juice
1½ envelopes of Sweet 'N Low
1-lb. can of whole beets, including the liquid
  (Use 6 ozs. of liquid and 6 ozs. of beets.
  Dice the beets. Reserve the balance
  of the liquid and beets for
  another meal.)

Season the chicken lightly with salt and pepper and place in a heavy dutch oven or casserole dish. Add the onions, onion flakes, garlic, curry powder, ginger, cooked-down tomato juice and water, and bring to a boil. Cook, uncovered, for 30 to 40 minutes on a low flame. Uncover and cook for approximately another 20 minutes. Add the beet liquid, diced beets, lemon juice and sweetener, and cook, uncovered, until the chicken is tender and the sauce has thickened.

This recipe will serve four at dinner only. The limited vegetable allowance for four persons is included—12ozs. of beets and beet juice and 4 ozs. of fresh onions.

NOTE: This is a lovely party dish—spicy to the taste and attractive to the eye! It can be made ahead and frozen.

CHICKEN IN BUTTERMILK

1 chicken, cut up
1 cup of buttermilk
1 tbsp. of dried chives
Salt and pepper, to taste
6 large mushrooms, sliced on a grater
Paprika

Place the chicken in a casserole and pour all of the other ingredients over it, except the paprika. Bake, covered, at 350° for 1 hour. Uncover the casserole and sprinkle the chicken with paprika. Bake, uncovered, for ½ hour longer, basting several times. Serve 4 ozs. for lunch; 6 ozs. for dinner.

The sauce looks white at the beginning but becomes clear when cooked!

CHICKEN IN ORANGE JUICE

2 chicken breasts
Salt, pepper and garlic powder, to taste
2 ozs. of orange juice
1 tsp. of KikkoMan Soy Sauce
½ envelope of Sweet 'N Low

Season the chicken well with salt, pepper and garlic powder and allow to stand for 10 minutes or more. Mix the orange juice, soy sauce and sweetener, and pour over the chicken. Marinate in the refrigerator for several hours, if possible; then, bake at 350°, covered, for 1 hour. Remove the cover and bake for about another 15 to 20 minutes until nicely browned on top. Serves 2 for dinner, or you can use it for lunch in 4-oz. portions.

NOTE: Count the orange juice as part of your daily

fruit allowance. If you don't want to use your fruit allowance, substitute 4 ozs. of Cott's Diet Orange Soda for the orange juice.

CHICKEN BREASTS WITH BEAN SPROUTS

2 chicken breasts, cut in half
2 cups of tomato juice
2 tbsps. dried onion flakes
¼ tsp. of sweet basil, crushed
¼ tsp. of oregano, crushed
⅛ tsp. of garlic powder
Salt and pepper to taste
Sprinkles of Sweet 'N Low
Few sprinkles of Parmesan cheese
2 cans of bean sprouts, drained and rinsed

Cook the tomato juice, uncovered, with the onion flakes, oregano, sweet basil, garlic powder, salt and pepper for about 10 minutes, until the mixture has thickened a great deal. Add the sweetener. Spread the bean sprouts on the bottom of a casserole dish. Season the chicken breasts with salt and pepper and place them on top of the bean sprouts. Spoon the cooked tomato sauce over the chicken and bake, uncovered, for 1 hour at 350°. Remove the casserole from the oven, sprinkle with a little Parmesan cheese, and broil for a few minutes. Serve 4-oz. portions for lunch; 6-oz. portions for dinner.

Remember to count the tomato juice toward your daily allowance!

CHICKEN AND EGGPLANT CASSEROLE

Chicken
2-3 lb. broiler-fryers, cut up

16 ozs. of cooked-down tomato juice
2 cloves of garlic, finely minced
2 to 4 envelopes of Sweet 'N Low
1 tsp. of salt
2 tbsps. Worcestershire Sauce
½ tsp. of paprika
2 tbsps. of white vinegar
½ tsp. of turmeric

Pre-heat the oven to 425°. Arrange the chicken in a large Teflon roasting pan, skin-side up. Bake, uncovered, for about 30 minutes, or until golden brown. You may add some water to the bottom of the pan, if desired. Reduce the heat to 350°.

While the chicken is roasting at 425°, place the tomato juice, garlic, salt, vinegar, turmeric, Worcestershire Sauce and paprika in a saucepan and simmer, uncovered, for 10 minutes. Add the sweetener, to taste, starting with 2 envelopes of Sweet 'N Low. Spoon 1 cup of this sauce over the chicken, coating all of the pieces, and return to the 350° oven, uncovered, for 20 minutes, or until tender. Add the diced onions and diced green pepper to the rest of the sauce, and simmer, **covered**, for 10 minutes, or until the vegetables are tender.

Eggplant
Medium-sized eggplant
4 medium onions, diced
1 large green pepper, diced
1 envelope MBT Chicken Broth
8 ozs. of water

Peel and cut the eggplant into strips about 1½" wide and ¼ to ½" thick. With broth and water mixed together, cook the eggplant until fork-tender, removing from the pan as each layer is cooked.

After the chicken has finished baking, arrange the eggplant on top of the chicken. Then, pour the balance of the sauce over the eggplant. Return pan to the oven and bake, uncovered, at 350° for 15 minutes. Serves 4 or 5 for dinner.

This is time-consuming to make but freezes beautifully! I served this to dieters at a dinner party and it was a big hit!

Count the eggplant and onions as limited dinner vegetables. If the onions and peeled eggplant exceed the allowed weight for limited vegetables, substitute onion flakes for part of the diced onion required.

ROASTED TURKEY BREAST

Frozen turkey breast, thawed
Salt, pepper, garlic powder and paprika, to taste

Season the breast well and allow to stay in the refrigerator for several hours. When ready to bake, line your roasting pan with a large sheet of heavy duty foil and place the turkey, breast-side down, on the foil. Cover, making a tight packet of the foil. Bake for the time suggested in instructions which come with the turkey, at 325°. About ½ hour before the turkey breast should be done, open the packet, raise the heat to 375°, and turn the breast over. Bake for 30 minutes longer.

Use leftover turkey to make Turkey à La King (see Elegant Chicken a La King on pp. 73-73) or Turkey and Chinese Vegetables (see Chinese Chicken and Vegetables on pp. 79-80).

Fish and Shellfish

Make a good friend of fish and shellfish! Remember that fish is a great source of protein, low in calories and generally lower in cost than other proteins!

Since you will be eating fish five times weekly, learn to be creative so you won't become easily bored.

Use fish soups once or twice weekly, make a cold fish salad with leftovers, and by all means, try the Baked Fish in Clam-Mushroom Sauce or Baked Fish Creole for dinner. Ask the family members to try your appetizing fish dishes (and they are just that!) and I'm sure you'll have some converts to fish eating!

If you have a freezer, do as I do. Freeze anything freezable on these pages. It will make your life easier! For example, if your family is having a pork meal, it would be very simple to pull out a pre-weighed portion of fish for yourself. No extra work! No fuss! No mess!!

CREAMED TUNA BAKE

½ package french-cut, cooked string beans
   or broccoli, cauliflower, or any
   combination of unlimited vegetables
3 ozs. of water
1 envelope MBT Chicken Broth

½ tbsp. dried onion flakes, or more
4 ozs. of tuna fish, drained and flaked
1 4-oz. can of mushrooms, including the liquid
2 to 3 tbsps. of powdered skimmed milk
1 slice of enriched white bread,
    toasted and blended into crumbs
Salt, pepper and dill weed, to taste

Place the powdered milk, water, liquid from the mushrooms, onion flakes and ½ can of mushrooms as well as the broth, in a blender. Whirl until smooth.

Arrange ½ of the bread crumbs on the bottom of a Teflon loaf pan (7⅜″ x 3⅝″ x 2¼″) or a small glass casserole dish. Spread the tuna, vegetables, remaining mushrooms, little salt, several sprinkles of pepper and several shakes of dill weed on top. Pour the blended liquid mixture over and sprinkle the remaining bread crumbs on top. Bake, uncovered, at 350° for 45 to 60 minutes. Serves 1 for lunch.

Remember to count the milk toward your daily allowance.

CREAMED TUNA FISH ON TOAST

4 ozs. tuna fish, drained
2 ozs. of evaporated skimmed milk
3 tbsps. of cut-up green pepper,
    or ½ of a small pepper
1 Progresso Roasted Pepper
1 tsp. dried onion flakes
Scant sprinklings of salt and pepper
Several pinches of dill weed
1 slice of white enriched bread, toasted

Place the milk, green pepper, roasted pepper, onion flakes and dill weed in a blender and run on "low" speed for about 1 minute. Pour into a saucepan and add the tuna fish, salt and pepper (if desired), and simmer for a minute or two. Pour over one slice of toast.

NOTE: Count 2 ozs. of evaporated skimmed milk as ¼ of your daily milk allowance. This is a simple-to-make fish lunch. To make this into a dinner meal, add 1 more oz. of evaporated skimmed milk, 2 more ozs. of tuna fish, and 4 ozs. of cooked peas. Remember: No bread at dinner!

TUNA FISH AND ROASTED PEPPERS

4 ozs. of tuna fish
⅓ jar of roasted peppers and a little liquid
1 tsp. of freeze-dried chives or
    dried onion flakes

Place all of the ingredients in a blender and run on "low" speed just until it's mixed through. If allowed to remain in the blender, it will be like a paté.

SALMON AND FILLET ROLLS

1 lb. fillet sole
1-lb. can salmon
1 tbsp. dried onion flakes, or more
1 tbsp. vegetable flakes, or more
1 tsp. mild prepared mustard
Sprinkling of pepper
Several drops of Worcestershire Sauce
1 cup tomato juice, or more

Wash the fish and divide through the center the long way, taking out the small line of practically invisible bones. Mix the salmon with 1 tbsp. of onion flakes, 1 tbsp. of dried vegetable flakes, 1 tsp. of mustard, 2 tbsps. of tomato juice and several shakes of pepper. Roll the fillets around the salmon (like stuffing). In the bottom of a baking pan, pour 1 cup of tomato juice, small amounts of dried onion and vegetable flakes, several sprinkles of Worcestershire Sauce, and fit the rolls in the pan snugly. Bake, uncovered, at 350° for ¾ hour. Baste the fish two or three times while baking.

Serve 4-oz. portions for lunch; 6-oz. portions for dinner.

Count the tomato juice toward your daily allowance.

SALMON CROQUETTES

8 ozs. of canned red salmon
1 slice of enriched white bread
1 4-oz. can of sliced mushrooms,
  including liquid
½ green pepper, diced
4 tbsps. of water
2 tbsps. of powdered skimmed milk
Sprinkles of pepper

Place the bread in a blender and run until you have soft bread crumbs. Place the liquid from the mushrooms in a pan and add the green pepper, and onion flakes, and cook down quickly until the liquid evaporates. Mix the breadcrumbs with the salmon, green pepper, onion flakes, mushrooms, pepper, powdered milk and water. Shape into patties and fry in a pre-heated Teflon skillet until browned. Turn patties over and brown on other side. This will serve two for lunch.

NOTE: You can supplement lunch with ½ slice of bread per person.

SPICY SALMON ON TOAST

4 ozs. of canned salmon, flaked
½ tbsp. of dried onion flakes
6 to 8 ozs. of tomato juice
1 tsp. Worcestershire Sauce
1 slice of white toast

Cook the onion flakes in tomato juice and Worcestershire Sauce, uncovered, for a few minutes. Add the salmon and heat through. Serve on toast. Serves 1 for lunch.

Variation: Add 2 ozs. of mushrooms, sliced, and 2 tbsps. of chopped green pepper to tomato juice and stew with flakes.

Remember to count the tomato juice toward your daily allowance.

SALMON AND PEAS EN CASSEROLE

12 ozs. of red canned salmon
8 ozs. of frozen peas, uncooked
2 tbsps. dried onion flakes
4 ozs. of liquified skimmed milk
4-oz. can of mushrooms, drained
Sprinkles of salt and pepper

Mix all the above ingredients together and pack into

a Teflon junior loaf pan. Bake uncovered at 375° for 1 hour. This is a dinner meal for 2 and includes limited dinner vegetables for 2.

NOTE: You may use the drained mushroom liquid in making up the skimmed milk. If you like your salmon spicy, add some prepared mustard before baking.

BAKED FISH CREOLE

32 ozs. of tomato juice
1 large green pepper
2 tbsps. of dried vegetable flakes
2 tbsps. of dried onion flakes
Several pinches of oregano
Pinch of sweetener
Salt (optional as the fish is salty)
2 lbs. of turbot

Cook all of the above ingredients, except the fish, uncovered, for about 20 minutes, or until the sauce is thickened and the vegetables are soft. Spoon the sauce over the fish and bake at 350°, uncovered, for 30 minutes or longer. Serves 4 for dinner. You can serve this for lunch by using 4-oz. portions. This freezes very well.

Remember to count the tomato juice toward your daily allowance.

NOTE: The sauce can be frozen separately without juice toward your daily allowance.

SALMON LOAF

1-lb. can red salmon
1 rounded tbsp. dried onion flakes

3 tbsps. of diced green pepper
3 ozs. of skimmed milk
6 whole mushrooms, cut up, or
  ½ small can of sliced mushrooms
1 tsp. of prepared mustard
Sprinkle of pepper
Several sprinkles of dill weed (optional)

Mix all of the above ingredients together and bake in a Teflon junior loaf pan for about 1 hour at 375°.

This will serve 2 for dinner or 3 for lunch.

If using canned mushrooms, reserve the liquid and use to reconstitute the powdered skimmed milk!

SALMON MOUSSE

1-lb. can red salmon, drained and flaked
½ cup of diced celery
½ cup of diced green pepper
1 tbsp. dried onion flakes
2 tbsps. lemon juice
⅛ tsp. of dill weed
2 tsps. of **toasted** sesame seeds (optional)
1 cup of tomato juice
2 envelopes of Knox Unflavored Gelatin
1 cup of buttermilk
½ envelope of Sweet 'N Low
Salt and pepper, to taste

Soften the gelatin in ½ cup of tomato juice. Add the other half of the tomato juice and bring to a boil to dissolve the gelatin. Allow to cool; then, add all of the other ingredients. Refrigerate until syrupy. Then, spoon the mixture into a mold and refrigerate for several hours . . . preferably overnight.

Unmold on lettuce leaves and garnish with sliced cucumbers. This will serve four for lunch.

Variation: You can use tuna fish or cold, leftover fish instead of salmon, and follow directions as given above.

NOTE: I do not recommend this for an evening meal since the portion would be too much to eat.

BAKED FISH WITH MUSHROOM SAUCE

1½ lb. fillet of sole or haddock
  (if sole is used, layer the fish as it is thin)
1 4-oz. can of sliced mushrooms and liquid
  (reserve half of the mushrooms)
2 tbsps. of powdered skimmed milk
Salt and pepper, to taste
1 tbsp. of dried onion flakes
Sprinkles of garlic powder and paprika

Place the mushrooms, liquid, milk, salt, pepper, garlic powder and onion flakes in a blender. Blend until smooth. Spread this mixture on the fish and add the reserved mushroom slices. Sprinkle with paprika and bake, uncovered, at 400° for 20 to 30 minutes, or until the fish flakes. Serve 4-oz. portions for lunch; 6-oz. portions for dinner.

Remember to count the milk toward your daily allowance.

Varation: Add dill weed or chives to top before baking.

BAKED FISH IN CLAM-MUSHROOM SAUCE

¼ lb. of fresh mushrooms, sliced

1 lb. turbot (Greenland halibut fillet)
McCormick's Season-All
Dill weed
2 to 3 tbsps. of clam juice
Paprika
Lemon wedges
Pepper to taste (do not add salt
 as the clam juice is salty)

Place the fish in a low casserole dish. Sprinkle it with clam juice, McCormick's Season-All, dill weed and pepper; then, top with mushrooms. Bake uncovered at 350° for 15 to 20 minutes. Remove the casserole from the oven and sprinkle liberally with paprika. Return dish to the oven for 10 to 15 minutes, depending upon the thickness of the fish. Baste with pan juices several times during the last 10 to 15 minutes. Serve with lemon wedges. The recipe will serve 2 for dinner; almost 3 for lunch! This freezes well.

BAKED HALIBUT

1 lb. halibut
2 stalks of celery, cut up
8 ozs. of carrots, cut up
1 tbsp. dried onion flakes
½ envelope MBT Vegetable Broth
Salt and pepper to taste
¾ cup of water
½ of a 4-oz. can of mushrooms, and liquid

Cook all of the ingredients, except the fish, for about 8 minutes, until the liquid has cooked down some and the vegetables are half-cooked. Place the fish in the bottom of a casserole dish, pour the vegetables and liquid over the fish, and bake uncovered at 350° for 20 mintues. Sprinkle paprika on top and bake for 10 to 15 minutes longer. This recipe will serve 2 (for dinner only). This freezes well!

MARINATED SWORDFISH

1 tbsp. of lemon juice
1 tbsp. of orange juice
2 tbsps. of KikkoMan Soy Sauce
1 tbsp. of tomato juice
Sprinkles of garlic powder and oregano
1 tbsp. of fresh parsley,
   or ¼ tsp. of parsley flakes
Pinch of Sweet 'N Low
1 lb. fresh swordfish, about 1" thick

Combine all of the ingredients in a shallow dish and add the fish. Marinate for several hours, turning the fish frequently. Remove fish from the marinade and broil it 3 inches from the heat for 5 minutes on each side.

Serve 4-oz. portions for lunch; 6-oz. portions for dinner!

SWORDFISH STEAK WITH SAUCE

1½ lbs. of swordfish
4 ozs. of chopped onion
8 ozs. of tomato, cut up
1 large green pepper, coarsely diced
Salt, pepper and sweet basil, to taste

In Teflon skillet saute the onion, tomato and pepper until soft. Add some water to make the sauce (or add water during cooking, if the sauce is thin). Season to taste with salt, freshly ground pepper and basil.

Salt and pepper the fish lightly. Pour the sauce over the fish and bake, uncovered, for 35 to 45 minutes in a 350° oven, until the fish flakes easily. Serves 3 for dinner.

NOTE: Weigh the fish portions without the sauce. The sauce contains limited dinner vegetable.

Variation: Add mushrooms.

BROILED SWORDFISH

8 ozs. fresh swordfish
Several tbsps. of KikkoMan Soy Sauce
Dill weed

Marinate the swordfish in soy sauce for several hours in the refrigerator, turning the fish occasionally. Drain and broil the fish for several minutes on one side. Turn the fish over and sprinkle dill weed on top. Broil at high heat for a few minutes until the fish is crusty and brown. This recipe will serve 1 for dinner.

This can be made in larger quantities and frozen. Leftover fish is delicious cold with a sauce (pp. 147-152).

COLD FISH SALAD

6 ozs. turbot (Greenland halibut fillet)
4 ozs. buttermilk
½ tsp. dry Good Seasons Low-Calorie Italian

Dressing (more or less)
Paprika

Place the fish in a baking dish and cover with buttermilk which has been mixed with dry salad dressing. Bake, uncovered, at 350° for about 20 minutes, or until the fish is cooked. (You may add more buttermilk if needed.) After about 10 minutes in the oven, remove the fish and baste. Then, sprinkle with paprika and return to the oven to finish cooking. Allow the fish to cool and mash it with a fork, using sauce to moisten. Refrigerate for 1 hour or so. (This is also very good served hot and not mashed!)

This recipe will serve one for Lunch. If you wish to serve this for Dinner, increase the protein to 8 ozs., buttermilk to 5 ozs. and powdered salad dressing to ¾ tsp. Be sure to count the buttermilk toward your daily milk allowance.

PICKLED FISH

2 lbs. of fish, thick and firm
　　(swordfish or other)
3 cups of water
1 cup of white vinegar
2 tbsps. of pickling spices
1 bay leaf
3 lemon slices
4 to 8 envelopes of Sweet 'N Low
3 onions, cut up

Simmer all of the above ingredients, except the fish and sweetener, for ½ hour. Remove the bay leaf after the first 10 minutes. Strain the marinade and then

simmer, covered, with the fish for 10 to 12 minutes.
Add the sweetener, to taste. Chill the fish, in the
marinade, in your refrigerator. Serve 4-oz. portions for
lunch; 6-oz. portions for dinner.

COLD HALIBUT SALAD

Fish
2 lbs. halibut steak
1 bay leaf
Juice of ½ lemon
Water to cover

Dressing
6 ozs. of Good Season's Low-Calorie
   Italian Salad Dressing
½ cup of diced celery
1 tbsp. of mild prepared mustard
1 pimiento, diced

Simmer fish with the bay leaf, lemon juice and water
for about 15 minutes, until the fish flakes easily and is
white in color. Cool and remove the fish from the liquid. Flake the fish and mix with the celery, salad
dressing, pimiento and mustard. Correct seasonings
since you may want to add salt and pepper. Serve this
on a large lettuce leaf with cucumber slices around the
salad. Serve 4-oz. portions for lunch; 6-oz. portions for
dinner!

This fish will stay in the refrigerator for several days.
To make a 6-oz. portion of fish salad, use 3 tbsps. of
salad dressing, 1 tsp. of mustard, and 1 tbsp. of diced
celery.

Try other sauces on this fish (pp. 147-152).

COD FISH STEW

6 or 8 ozs. of fillet of cod or
    fillet of haddock
1 tbsp. of dried vegetable flakes
1 tbsp. of dried onion flakes
6 ozs. of clam juice
6 ozs. of tomato juice or Clamato juice
2 envelope MBT Chicken Broth
Several drops of Worcestershire Sauce
½ cup of diced celery
1 green pepper, diced
Fresh dill (optional)
Salt and pepper to taste

Simmer all of the ingredients, uncovered, except the fish, for about 3 to 5 minutes. Add the fish, cut up in pieces, and simmer for a few more minutes. This recipe will serve 1 for lunch or dinner.

NOTE: A 6-oz. portion of raw fish equals 4 ozs. cooked, for lunch; an 8-oz. portion of raw fish equals 6 ozs. cooked, for dinner.

Variation: You may wish to use reconstituted skimmed milk instead of the tomato juice for New England Style Stew.

BAKED CHILI-CRAB

8 ozs. of frozen or canned crabmeat, flaked
3 ozs. of celery, diced fine
1 slice of enriched white bread
1½ tbsps. of dried onion flakes
6 ozs. "Legal" Chili Sauce (p. 151)

(Use pumpkin pie spice in
   making this recipe)
1 tsp. of salt
2 to 3 ozs. of water

Sauté celery and onion flakes in 2 to 3 ozs. of water until the vegetables are soft and the liquid evaporates. Bake the bread in a 250° oven for about 10 to 15 minutes, until dried out. Break up the bread and place in a blender to make crumbs. Add the Chili Sauce and bread crumbs to the celery-onion mixture and toss lightly. Add salt and flaked crabmeat. Stuff into clam shells and bake, uncovered, in a 300° pre-heated oven for 25 to 30 minutes.

Be sure to eat the additional ½ slice of bread each to make up your lunch allowance; the recipe only calls for 1 slice for 2 servings!

BROILED SCALLOPS

1¼ lbs. of bay scallops
   (or sea scallops cut in half)
¼ envelope of Good Seasons Low Calorie
   Italian Salad Dressing Mix (dry)
Dill weed

Wash and dry the scallops and spread in a baking dish. Sprinkle the dry salad dressing mix lightly over the scallops, and then sprinkle the dill weed on top. Broil for 5 minutes. Weigh portions after cooking as scallops shrink a good deal.

Serve 4-oz. portions for lunch; 6-oz. portions for dinner.

SCALLOPS WITH DILL #1

10 ozs. of scallops, raw
2 to 3 tbsps. of KikkoMan Soy Sauce
Italian Salad Dressing Mix (dry)
Dill Weed

Wash and dry the scallops and spread in a baking dish. Sprinkle the dry salad dressing mix lightly over the scallops, and then sprinkle the dill weed on top. Broil for 5 minutes. Weigh portions after cooking as scallops shrink a good deal.

Serve 4-oz. portions for lunch; 6-oz. portions for dinner.

SCALLOPS WITH DILL #2

10 ozs. of scallops, raw
2 to 3 tbsps. of KikkoMan Soy Sauce
1 tbsp. of lemon juice
Sprinkles of garlic powder
Sprinkles of dill weed

Mix soy sauce, lemon juice and garlic powder, and brush on the scallops with a pastry brush. Allow to marinate in the refrigerator for 30 minutes, or longer. Sprinkle liberally with dill weed and bake, uncovered, at 350° for about 15 minutes. If using bay scallops, shorten the baking time slightly.

NOTE: Scallops shrink a great deal in cooking. Weigh 6-oz. portions after cooking.

CREAMED SCALLOPS AND MUSHROOMS

10 ozs. of bay scallops or cut-up sea scallops

4-oz. can of sliced mushrooms, including liquid
2 tbsps. of powdered skimmed milk
Salt, pepper and paprika, to taste
Several shakes of dill weed
Sprinkling of Parmesan cheese

In a Teflon skillet mix the liquid from the mushrooms (about ¼ cup) and powdered skimmed milk. Add salt, pepper, paprika and several shakes of dill weed. Mix well; then, add the scallops and cook for about 5 minutes, covered. Add the mushrooms, Parmesan cheese, and warm through. If there is too much liquid in the pan, cook down on high flame with the cover off. Serve over asparagus or cooked cauliflower.

NOTE: Scallops shrink a great deal in cooking. Measure 10 ozs. raw for dinner; 8 ozs. raw for lunch. Count the milk toward your daily allowance!

SCALLOPS IN TOMATO SAUCE

10 ozs. of bay scallops, or cut-up sea scallops
4 ozs. of tomato juice
1 tbsp. Worcestershire Sauce
Sprinkles of garlic powder
2 ozs. dried diced onion, or 1 tbsp. onion flakes
Pinch of Sweet 'N Low

Steam all of the above in a covered skillet until thickened, 10 to 15 minutes. Then, remove the cover and allow the sauce to cook down.

This recipe will serve 1 for dinner. Scallops shrink a great deal in cooking. Therefore, measure 10 ozs. raw for dinner; 8 ozs. raw for lunch.

NOTE: If you are using a whole onion, remember this is half of a limited vegetable. Be sure to count tomato juice toward your daily allowance.

You may use this recipe for lunch if dried onion flakes are used instead of fresh onion, and the scallops are 8 ozs. raw weight.

SMALL BROILED LOBSTER TAILS

10 ozs. baby lobster tails
½ small onion, or less, grated
Garlic powder, salt, pepper and oregano,
   to taste

Slit the shell of the baby lobster tails and grate the onion over each tail. Season lightly with garlic powder, salt, pepper and oregano, and broil for about 10 minutes. Serves 1 for dinner.

NOTE: Consider the grated onion as part of limited dinner vegetable!

Variations: After minutes of broiling time, spoon on sauce, pre-cooked, made of tomatoes, diced onions, diced peppers, salt, pepper and basil. This is quite spicy.

Eggs and Cheese

Remember, eggs and cheese are breakfast and lunch foods only, and are not to be used in snacks, etc.

Here's an opportunity to try my very favorite recipe, Elegant Bread Pudding! Precede it with a Scrambled Egg with Chives and Mushrooms, a Deviled Egg, or Confetti Egg Salad made from one egg. Invite your friends to lunch; it's certain you'll make a big hit!

ELEGANT BREAD PUDDING

1 slice enriched white bread, toasted
½ cup of liquified skimmed milk
1 medium-sized baking apple
   (Rome Beauty, preferably)
1 egg, slightly beaten
1 tbsp. of cinnamon and Sweet 'N Low mixture
   (p. 10)
1 cap of vanilla or almond extract
Nutmeg
1 envelope of Sweet 'N Low

Peel the apple and slice very thin. Cut the bread into small croutons. Mix 1 tbsp. of cinnamon and sweetener mixture with the apple slices, and toss well. Set aside.

Beat the egg with a fork, add milk, vanilla extract, several sprinkles of nutmeg and 1 envelope of Sweet 'N Low.

Line a Teflon junior loaf pan with ½ of bread croutons and then make a layer of ½ of the apple mixture. The next layer will be the balance of bread croutons, and the top layer will be the balance of the apple mixture. Pour the egg mixture over all and bake, uncovered, for 1 hour in a pre-heated 350° oven.

This recipe will serve 1 for breakfast or part of lunch. Count this as your bread allowance for either meal. This is also ½ cup of your daily milk allowance, 1 egg and 1 fruit.

NOTE: This can be made in a low casserole in larger amounts, cut into allowed portions and frozen individually for breakfast or lunch. It's best made fresh, however.

CONFETTI EGG SALAD

2 hard-boiled eggs
2 ozs. of canned mushrooms,
    drained and diced
3 tbsps. of green pepper, diced fine,
    or 1½ tbsps. of green pepper and
    1½ tbsps. of red pepper
2 tbsps. of celery, diced fine
1 tsp. dried onion flakes
¼ tsp. of salt
Sprinkles of pepper
1 oz. of buttermilk
¼ tsp. of mild prepared mustard
1 tsp. of capers, drained
Pinch of sweetener

Mash the eggs and add the mushrooms, green (or green and red) pepper, celery, onion flakes, salt and pepper. Mix the buttermilk, mustard, capers and sweetener together. Mix the egg and buttermilk mixtures together, and chill.

This will serve 2 for breakfast or 1 for lunch. If you eat half of this at lunch, you can follow it with my Elegant Bread Pudding (p. 105) which will use the other egg for your lunch meal.

Remember to count the buttermilk toward your daily milk allowance.

SPEEDY EGG SALAD

2 ozs. of diced celery
2 hard-boiled eggs
1 tbsp. of powdered skimmed milk
2 tbsps. of water
1 tsp. of prepared mild mustard
1 tsp. dried onion flakes (optional)

Mix the powdered milk with the water to make a loose paste. Add the mustard and onion flakes. Mash the eggs and add the other ingredients, mixing thoroughly. Refrigerate for 10 to 20 minutes, if possible, for the flavors to blend.

This will serve 1 for lunch.

SCRAMBLED EGGS WITH CHIVES AND MUSHROOMS

½ can of sliced mushrooms, drained
2 eggs, beaten

1 tbsp. of fresh chives (or frozen)
⅛ tsp. of shallots (optional)
1 cap of KikkoMan Soy Sauce
Salt and pepper to taste

Combine all of the above and fry in a Teflon pan. This will serve 1 for lunch or 2 for breakfast.

Use half of this recipe if you are planning to follow this with the Elegant Bread Pudding (p. 105) at lunch.

DEVILED EGGS

2 hard-boiled eggs
1 tsp. of prepared mild mustard
1½ tbsps. of buttermilk,
    or evaporated skimmed milk
1 tsp. dried onion flakes
⅛ tsp. of salt
Sprinkle of pepper
⅛ tsp. of celery seed
Paprika

Cut the hard-boiled eggs in half and remove the yolks. Mix the rest of the ingredients together, except the paprika, and mash the yolks, adding them to this mixture. Stuff back into the egg whites and sprinkle with paprika. Refrigerate for ½ hour or longer.

This recipe will serve 1 for lunch. You may use this for breakfast. If you have the Elegant Bread Pudding (p. 105) for lunch, you may use 1 Deviled Egg to supplement 1 egg in the Elegant Bread Pudding. (Only half of this recipe can be used for breakfast.)

MOCK CHOPPED LIVER

2 hard-boiled eggs
1 4-oz. can of mushrooms, and liquid
4 ozs. of french-cut string beans,
   freshly cooked and drained
1 envelope MBT Chicken Broth
1 tsp. dried onion flakes
Pepper, to taste

Mash the eggs. Place eggs, string beans and mushroom liquid, as well as the broth (dry), in a blender. Run for 30 seconds. Add the mushrooms and blend for an additional few seconds. Add dried onion flakes and freshly ground pepper, to taste. Refrigerate.

Since this is bland in color, garnish with parsley and sliced pimiento on top. This recipe will serve half of breakfast or 1 complete lunch.

SPINACH SOUFFLÉ

½ cup of spinach, chopped, cooked and drained
½ cup of skimmed milk
1 egg
½ tsp. dried onion flakes, crushed
Salt and pepper to taste

Blend the spinach and milk. Beat the egg and stir in spinach, milk, onion flakes and seasonings. Pour into a Teflon junior loaf pan and bake, uncovered, at 350° until set, about 30 to 40 minutes. . .or when a silver knife comes out clean.

This will serve half of lunch.

Variation: Asparagus Soufflé! Instead of spinach, use ½ cup of cut-up drained, cooked asparagus. Proceed as above.

EGG FOO YUNG SOUFFLÉ

½ green pepper, diced
½ stalk of celery, diced (optional)
1 tbsp. of dried onion flakes
½ cup of bean sprouts, drained
1 envelope MBT Chicken Broth
1 cup of water
1 tsp. of KikkoMan Soy Sauce
⅛ tsp. of salt (optional)
Sprinkle of pepper
1 tbsp. freeze-dried chives
2 eggs, beaten

Bring water to a boil in the skillet. Add the broth, green pepper, celery, onion flakes and ½ tsp. of soy sauce. Cook quickly, uncovered, until almost all of the liquid has cooked down and the vegetables are softened. Add the chives and drained bean sprouts, and cook quickly until all of the liquid has cooked away.

Beat the eggs with a fork. Add salt (optional) and pepper and the other ½ tsp. of soy sauce. Beat with a fork for a minute. Add the softened vegetable mixture to the eggs and turn into a Teflon junior loaf pan.

Bake uncovered in a pre-heated 350° oven for 30 minutes. Remove pan from the oven and loosen the sides with a Teflon spatula. Turn over on a dish. This is beautifully browned and very eye-appealing, too!

If you are serving 2 persons for lunch, double the

recipe and use a Teflon pie plate to bake. If you want to serve Elegant Bread Pudding with this dish, eat only half of this recipe which allows for 1 egg. (The Elegant Bread Pudding is made with an egg also.)

If you prefer, you may make Egg Foo Yung by heating a Teflon skillet and dropping the mixture by spoon, in pancake size. Do not turn until the bottom of the pancake is browned!

GRILLED CHEESE WITH CUCUMBERS

1 slice of enriched white bread
2 ozs. of Muenster cheese, plain or caraway
Ehler's Sauté Onion Powder
½ peeled cucumber, sliced thin
Salt

Toast the bread and slice through the middle to make two thin slices. Place bread on the broiler pan, cut-side up; then, place 1 oz. slice of cheese on each piece of toast. Sprinkle generously with Ehler's Sauté Onion Powder and place under the broiler until brown and bubbly. Serve with cucumber slices on top of the cheese, and sprinkle salt to taste.

This recipe will serve 1 for lunch. If you wish to use this for breakfast, use 1 oz. of cheese, but break it up and crumble over the cut sides of toasted bread. Top with onion powder. The cheese will spread to fill the slices as heat melts it.

VEGETABLES WITH CHEESE SAUCE

1 pkg. of broccoli, asparagus or french-cut
    string beans, cooked (or a combination

of unlimited cooked vegetables)
Ehler's Sauté Onion Powder
1 oz. Muenster cheese with caraway seeds

Arrange the vegetables in a pan and crumble the cheese on top of the vegetables. Sprinkle with Sauté Onion Powder and bake for a few minutes. Then broil for a few minutes—it will bubble and brown.

NOTE: Use another slice of cheese melted on white toast for a filling lunch as this recipe is only half of your lunch protein.

VEGETABLE-COTTAGE CHEESE

8-oz. container of cottage cheese
1 tbsp. of dehydrated vegetable flakes
½ tsp. of freeze-dried chives
½ tsp. dried onion flakes
2 tbsps. of water, cold or hot
Salt and pepper, to taste

Soften the vegetable flakes, chives and onion flakes in water. Allow to stand until all of the liquid has been absorbed by the flakes. Add a little salt and pepper to taste and mix through the cottage cheese.

This can be used in 2-oz. portions for breakfast, or 2/3 cup for lunch!

PIZZA

1 slice enriched white bread, toasted
2 ozs. Caraway-Muenster cheese
2 to 3 tbsps. of cooked-down tomato juice
Garlic powder

Oregano
Salt (optional)

Slice through the bread with a serrated knife to make two thin slices. Place bread in a pan, cut-side up. Place 1 slice of cheese on each piece of bread. Spoon cooked-down tomato juice on top. Sprinkle with garlic powder and oregano (which you have rubbed between your fingers to release the flavor). Top-brown in Toaster Oven or broiler until bubbly and nicely browned.

You may serve this at lunch only. If you're daring at breakfast, have this . . . but use 1 oz. of cheese only.

APPLE-CHEESE "PIE"

1 slice enriched white bread
1 Baked Apple and syrup (p. 169)
2 ozs. cottage cheese
Cinnamon and Sweet 'N Low mixture (p. 10)
1 tsp. Cranberry Conserve (p. 158)

Toast the bread. Place the bread in the bottom of a small baking dish. Put Baked Apple on top of the bread and mash the apple flat with a fork. Add syrup from the apples. Top with cottage cheese and spread the Cranberry relish on top of the cottage cheese. Sprinkle generously with the cinnamon and sweetener mixture.

Bake in a 350° pre-heated oven for 10 to 15 minutes. Then broil, or top-brown in a Toaster Oven until browned.

This is a delicious, filling breakfast and can be used for lunch if the balance of cottage cheese is eaten. Remember to count the apples as 1 fruit.

Variations: Peach or Pineapple Cheese Pie! Peel and

slice 1 peach. Cook for a few minutes in Cott's Black Cherry Diet Soda. ¼ of pineapple may be prepared this way also. After the fruit is soft and the liquid is reduced, complete the recipe as indicated above.

SISTER SARA'S "RHUBARB PIE"

1 slice enriched white bread, toasted
2 ozs. of cottage cheese
4 ozs. Rhubarb Conserve (p. 157)
Cinnamon and Sweet 'N Low mixture

Place the toast in a small pan. Add the cottage cheese, and layer with Rhubarb Conserve. Sprinkle liberally with the cinnamon-sweetener mixture and bake at 350° for 10 minutes. Then broil until the top is brown.

This recipe serves 1 for breakfast. If you want to use this for lunch, use the balance of cottage cheese with a salad. This pie is great with coffee!

Vegetables

Unlimited vegetables should always be available for you at meal time and in between. Have Pickled Cucumbers, Zucchini Vinaigrette, Cold Broccoli, Sweet and Sour Red Cabbage, or Cole Slaw with Celery Seeds on hand in the refrigerator so that you will not feel the need to nibble forbidden foods!

Limited vegetables are just that! They are eaten **only** at dinner, in 4-oz. portions. By planning your menus a few days in advance, you will be able to make large quantities and freeze them, or plan a limited vegetable that can stay refrigerated for some time!

Freeze 4-oz. portions of the Butternut Squash Casserole and it will be ready for you when you need it. This tastes very much like sweet potato and will become a favorite, I'm sure. Any of the Eggplant recipes or the Sweet and Sour Beets can be refrigerated for three or more days. Alternate your limited vegetables for variety!

NOTE: Pages 116 through 126 (except for Stewed Mushrooms and Onions on page 121) are unlimited vegetables and can be served at any time of day. All of the other recipes are limited.

COLD BROCCOLI ITALIAN STYLE

1 bunch of broccoli
Juice of ½ lemon
McCormick's Season-All Powder
Salt and pepper to taste
Garlic powder

Cook the broccoli in salted water. Drain and allow
to cool. Squeeze the lemon juice over the broccoli and
season generously with garlic powder and Season-All.
Then, season to taste with salt and pepper. Refrigerate
and turn several times. Serves 4.

COLD MUSHROOM-CUCUMBER SALAD

3 cucumbers, scrubbed, scored with a
    fork, and sliced thin
½ to ¾ lb. of fresh raw mushrooms, sliced
1½ to 2 tsps. of **toasted** sesame seeds
2 tsps. of KikkoMan Soy Sauce
1 tsp. of salt
4 tbsps. of mild wine vinegar
2 envelopes of Sweet 'N Low

Dissolve the sweetener in wine vinegar and add all of
the other seasonings. Toss with cucumbers and
mushrooms and refrigerate. If you wish, you can garnish this with chopped scallion. It tastes best if you use
it the day it is made. Serves 6 to 8.

PICKLED CUCUMBERS

3 cucumbers, scrubbed but not peeled
1 large onion
Salt
5 ozs. of white vinegar
3 ozs. of water
3 envelopes of Sweet 'N Low
Pepper and several shakes of dill weed

Score the cucumbers with a fork and slice them very thin. Slice the onion in thin rings and separate. Arrange one layer of cucumbers and then a layer of onion rings, salting liberally on each layer. Allow to stand for 30 minutes. Sit a small dish over the cucumbers in a bowl and drain off the bitter liquid. Add vinegar, water, sweetener, pepper and dill weed. Refrigerate. This keeps well for several days in the refrigerator . . . and will serve 6.

CUCUMBER IN "CREAM"

1 cucumber, scrubbed and sliced
Several sprinkles of dill weed
Salt and pepper to taste
Buttermilk

Season cucumber slices with salt, pepper and dill weed; top with thick buttermilk. Remember to count the milk toward your daily allowance!

Variation: Slice cucumber, radishes and scallions and season with salt and pepper. Top with thick buttermilk. Scallions are a limited dinner vegetable.

FRESH ASPARAGUS

Break upper tender portion from the "woody" base. Wash well. Cook, covered, in a very small amount of boiling, salted water, for 10 to 15 minutes. (If the stal' are thick, split up the bottom about ½" for tenderness.,

COLESLAW WITH CELERY SEED

1 large cabbage, finely chopped
2 tbsps. dried onion flakes
½ tsp. of salt, or more
⅛ tsp. of pepper
1 tsp. of celery seed
½ tbsp. of liquid sweetener
½ cup wine vinegar
½ cup of water

Add all of the other ingredients to the chopped-up cabbage and toss. Refrigerate. Correct seasonings when chilled. You may add diced peppers, if you wish.

BOILED CABBAGE

1 head of cabbage, cut up in small pieces
2 envelopes MBT Vegetable Broth
2 tbsps. dried onion flakes
½ cup of water
Several sprinkles of garlic powder
Salt and pepper to taste

Place all of the above ingredients in a covered pan and cook until the cabbage is tender.

SWEET AND SOUR RED CABBAGE

1 medium red cabbage, cut up in small pieces
8 ozs. of tomato juice
½ lemon, more or less
1 pkg. of Sweet 'N Low (more, if needed)
Salt and pepper to taste

Cook the cabbage covered with the tomato juice. When the cabbage is cooked, add all of the other ingredients. Refrigerate. This can be frozen.

RED CABBAGE WITH DICED APPLES

1 small red cabbage, cut up in small pieces
1 apple, peeled, cored and diced
2 tbsps. dried onion flakes
2 tbsps. of lemon juice
⅛ tsp. allspice
½ envelope MBT Chicken Broth (dry)
½ tsp. of salt, or more
6 ozs. of water
Sprinkles of pepper
2 envelopes of Sweet 'N Low

Cook all of the above ingredients, except the sweetener, in a covered saucepan for 20 minutes, or until the cabbage is tender. Add the sweetener and correct the other seasonings (you may need more salt). This entire recipe contains 1 fruit.

MARINATED VEGETABLES

Asparagus, fresh or frozen, or
   String beans, french-cut

Salt, pepper and garlic powder, to taste
Juice of ½ lemon
Water

Cook the vegetables in a small amount of water (salted) until tender but still firm. Drain and allow to cool. Season with salt, pepper and garlic powder. Squeeze the lemon juice over the vegetables and refrigerate. This is marvelous at a cook-out. Try it!

FRESH MUSHROOM COCKTAIL

1 lb. large fresh mushrooms
Lemon juice
Seafood Cocktail Sauce (p. 147)
Lettuce leaves
Diced celery (optional)

Clean the mushrooms and slice down through them to make attractive slices. Dip each slice in lemon juice and drain. Serve on a bed of lettuce and add diced celery. Dip in cocktail sauce.

The cocktail sauce contains tomato juice which must be considered in your daily allowance.

STEAMED ITALIAN PEPPERS

8 light green Italian frying peppers
2 tbsps. dried onion flakes
4-oz. can of mushrooms, including the liquid
½ tsp. of salt, or more
⅛ tsp. of pepper (scant)
⅛ tsp. of garlic powder
⅛ tsp. of oregano, or more
Sprinkles of paprika (optional)

Steam all of the above in a covered pan (you may need to add several ounces of water) until the peppers are tender. If there is liquid in the bottom of the pan, remove the cover and cook down quickly. Correct seasonings.

This is excellent with steaks, chops, hamburgers or frankfurters cooked outdoors on the grill. After the meat has been cooked, top with Steamed Italian Peppers before eating.

Variation: Add red peppers for color.

STEWED MUSHROOMS AND ONIONS

8 ozs. of onions, diced
1 lb. fresh mushrooms, sliced
½ to ⅔ envelope MBT Chicken Broth
Garlic powder
Salt, pepper and paprika, to taste
½ cup of water

Stew the onion in water, uncovered, for a few minutes. Then, sprinkle broth, salt, pepper, garlic powder and paprika over the onion, and stir. Add sliced mushrooms and allow to simmer, uncovered, for a few minutes. If the liquid evaporates during cooking, add a little more water.

Since onions are a limited vegetable (the mushrooms are unlimited), this should be served at dinner only!

FRENCH-CUT WAX BEANS

1 lb. yellow wax beans
1 envelope MBT Chicken or Vegetable Broth
½ cup of water

Salt, pepper and McCormick's Season-All,
  to taste

French-cut the beans and cook, covered, for a few
minutes in broth and water. Season to taste. This is
delicious with spicy food. Serves 4 to 6.

ORIENTAL VEGETABLE MINGLE

2 pkgs. of french-style string beans, thawed
1 4-oz. can of mushrooms, including the liquid
2 to 3 envelopes MBT Chicken Broth
½ head of Chinese celery cabbage, sliced
Diced water chestnuts (optional)
2 to 3 caps KikkoMan soy sauce
½ envelope of Sweet 'N Low, more or less

Combine the mushroom liquid with the broth in a
Teflon frying pan. Bring to a boil and add string beans
and celery cabbage, and cook for a few minutes. Add
mushrooms, water chestnuts and seasonings. Serve
immediately so vegetables will remain firm. This recipe
will serve 4.

NOTE: Water chestnuts are limited.

MOCK MASHED POTATOES

2 pkgs. of frozen cauliflower
1 to 2 envelopes MBT Chicken Broth

Cook the cauliflower in water, as directed on the
package, with the broth. Place the cooked cauliflower
in a blender and add enough of the liquid from the pot
to moisten . . . to the consistency of mashed potatoes.

BAKED ZUCCHINI

2 tbsps. dried onion flakes
12 ozs. of tomato juice
⅛ tsp. of oregano
⅛ tsp. of garlic powder
Salt and pepper, to taste
4 to 6 zucchini, sliced
Sprinkle of Parmesan cheese (optional)

Simmer the onion flakes, tomato juice, oregano, garlic powder, salt and pepper, until the sauce is thickened. Place the zucchini in a casserole dish and pour the sauce over. Bake, covered, in a 350° oven for 20 minutes. Sprinkle Parmesan cheese (ONE sprinkle) on top and allow to bake, uncovered, for 10 minutes longer, or until zucchini is tender.

Count the tomato juice toward your daily allowance.

STEAMED CELERY CABBAGE

1 pkg. of Chinese celery cabbage
   (Stalk—12 to 15 ribs)
2 envelopes MBT Chicken Broth
Salt and pepper to taste
12 ozs. of water
KikkoMan Soy Sauce (optional)

Bring water, seasonings and broth to a boil. Place the cabbage on its side and slice down at 1″ intervals. Separate the pieces. Add the cabbage to the water, seasonings and broth and cook for about a minute or two. **Add** several drops of soy sauce to the pot, if desired. Drain and serve. This recipe will serve 2 persons.

FRENCH STYLE STRING BEANS WITH MUSHROOMS

1 lb. string beans, french-cut
¼ lb. fresh mushrooms, sliced
Onion flakes
2 tbsps. of McCormick's Season-All
  (optional)
Pepper and very little salt
½ envelope MBT Chicken Broth
Several ozs. of water

Cook string beans for several minutes, until firm, in a little water flavored with salt, pepper and Season-All. In a skillet, using 2 to 3 ozs. of water and broth, cook the mushrooms with dried onion flakes for a few minutes. If more water is desired, add it sparingly. Mix mushroom mixture into the string beans, and serve.

COLD ZUCCHINI RELISH

4 zucchini, washed, **not** peeled
¼ to ½ tsp. of salt, depending on
  the size of the zucchini
1 to 2 ozs. of lemon juice
½ envelope of Sweet 'N Low
Water

Grate raw zucchini on the second largest opening of a 4-sided grater. Add salt, pepper and lemon juice.

Place ½″ of water in bottom of a saucepan and add all of the ingredients except the sweetener. Cook, uncovered, for 5 to 6 minutes. All of the liquid should be cooked down. Add the sweetener and chill. This is very good with cold fish salad!

ZUCCHINI VINAIGRETTE

5 to 6 medium zucchini,
    sliced into strips like pickle slices
    and cut in half once
1 envelope of Good Seasons Low-Calorie
    Italian Mix
½ cup of wine vinegar
½ cup of water
1 tbsp. of freeze-dried chives
2 tbsps. of finely chopped green pepper
Italian parsley
Pimientos

Pour vinegar and water into a shaker bottle with dry salad dressing mix, and shake well. Add the chives, parsley and green pepper. Cook the zucchini in boiling, salted water until barely tender . . . about 2 minutes. Drain. Arrange in a shallow dish and pour the dressing mix over. Refrigerate. When serving, garnish with pimiento strips. This can stay in your refrigerator for three or four days . . . and will serve 6.

STUFFED ZUCCHINI

3 large zucchini (green squash)
1 4-oz. can of mushrooms, chopped

Sprinkling of Parmesan cheese
1 tsp. dried onion flakes
Salt, pepper, garlic powder, to taste
Sprinkling of oregano
Several tablespoons of cooked-down tomato
    juice seasoned with salt, pepper,
    oregano, garlic powder and crushed onion
    flakes, to taste

Cut zucchini in half the long way. With a small knife, cut out the seeded center and reserve pulp. Cook the squash and pulp in a small amount of salted water a few minutes until the squash is still quite firm. Drain. Cut up the pulp and chop the mushrooms; then, mix together, season with salt, pepper and garlic powder. Stuff the zucchini shells with the mixture and place in a baking dish. Spoon the seasoned, cooked-down tomato juice over all and sprinkle Parmesan cheese on top. Bake for 5 minutes to brown and melt the cheese, in a 375° oven. Serves 4 to 6.

CRUSTLESS PUMPKIN PIE

1 lb. can of unprepared pumpkin
1½ tbsps. of Sweet 'N Low, or more
2 tsps. pumpkin pie spice
2 egg whites, beaten stiff
Pinch of salt
2 to 4 ozs. of evaporated skimmed milk

Mix the pumpkin, sweetener, pumpkin pie spice, milk and salt well. Fold in egg whites, gently, and place in a Teflon or glass pie plate. Place the pie plate in a pan of hot water and bake in a pre-heated 350° oven for 40 to 45 minutes. Cool and refrigerate. Serves 4.

This is a delicious dinner dessert and can be made ahead as the pie will stay well in the refrigerator for four or five days. Remember that pumpkin is a limited vegetable to be served at dinner only; also, count the milk toward your daily milk allowance.

ACORN SQUASH

1 acorn squash, cut in half
Cinnamon and sweetener mixture (p. 10)
Water

Place the squash, with seeds removed, cut-side up in a casserole. Pour 1″ of water into casserole, around the bottom of the squash. Place 1 tbsp. of water in the cavity of each half of squash. Sprinkle the cut-side liberally with the cinnamon and sweetener mixture. Cover the pan and bake in a 350° oven for ¾ hour. When the squash is soft, uncover and bake 10 minutes longer.

This is attractive to serve with poultry or fish. A dinner portion is 4 ozs.!

COLD BEETS, SWEET AND SOUR

2 1-lb. cans of whole beets
  (reserve 1 tbsp. of liquid)
2 envelopes of Sweet 'N Low
3 tbsps. of white vinegar
2 tbsps. of white horseradish
Salt, to taste

Grate the beets on the long, stringy side of the grater.

Add sweetener, vinegar, horseradish and four sprinkles of salt. If you want the mixture more moist, add 1 tbsp. of beet liquid. Refrigerate and serve cold. Serve 4-oz. portions as this is a limited dinner vegetable!

NOTE: This will stay in the refrigerator five or six days.

BUTTERNUT SQUASH CASSEROLE

1 butternut squash (with a long neck)
2 tbsps. of orange juice
3 to 4 tbsps. of water
Cinnamon and Sweet 'N Low mixture (p. 10)
Orange and lemon rind, powdered
   (optional)

Peel the squash with a potato peeler. Place the squash on its side and slice to get circles of ¼″ thickness. Remove the seeds from the rounded end of squash. Place the juice and water on the bottom of a pie plate or casserole dish. Make layers of squash and sprinkle liberally with cinnamon and sweetener mixture between each layer as well as on the top.

Bake, covered, at 350° until the squash is soft . . . about 30 minutes. Uncover the pan and continue to bake for about 10 minutes longer. You may add the powdered orange and lemon rind these last 10 minutes.

NOTE: This is my favorite limited vegetable. It tastes so good and goes so well with chicken or turkey! Serve 4-oz. portions at dinner!

Two tbsps. of orange juice is used in this recipe, but since it serves about six portions, the juice used for each serving is negligible!

EGGPLANT STEW

1 medium eggplant, peeled, sliced and cubed
2 stalks of celery, sliced diagonally
2 green peppers, cut up
1 can of mushrooms and some liquid
1 cup of tomato juice
2 tbsps. dried onion flakes
¼ tsp. of oregano
1 clove of garlic, or garlic powder
Salt and pepper, to taste
1 envelope of Sweet 'N Low
Sprinkling of Parmesan cheese

Cook all of the ingredients, uncovered, in a Teflon pan for a few minutes. Then cover the pan and cook until the eggplant is just barely tender. (If the sauce is too thin, remove the vegetables and cook down for a few minutes on high fire.) Sprinkle with Parmesan cheese before serving.

NOTE: You can serve 5-oz. portions as some of the vegetables used are unlimited. Remember to count the tomato juice toward your daily allowance.

BRUSSELS SPROUTS WITH CARAWAY SEED

1 pkg. of frozen brussels sprouts
½ envelope of MBT Chicken Broth
6 ozs. of water
¼ to ½ tsp. of caraway seeds
¼ tsp. of salt
Sprinkles of pepper

Allow the vegetable to thaw partially. Place in a

saucepan and add the broth, water, caraway seeds, salt and pepper. Cook covered for 6 minutes, or until the sprouts are tender. This is a limited dinner vegetable.

COLD EGGPLANT SALAD

1 small eggplant, peeled and cut
   in large cubes
1 envelope of MBT Vegetable Broth
Small amount of water
1 tbsp. dried onion flakes
½ medium onion, diced
2 tbsps. of cooked-down tomato juice
Salt, pepper, garlic powder, paprika,
   all to taste
1 envelope of Sweet 'N Low

Cook the eggplant cubes in broth, ½″ of water and onion flakes until tender. Drain. Add onion, tomato juice, spices and sweetener. Refrigerate and serve cold.

This vegetable is limited to 4-oz. portions at dinner.

COLD EGGPLANT, ITALIAN STYLE

1 medium eggplant, peeled and cubed
½ cup of diced onions
2 cloves of garlic
2 medium-ripe tomatoes, peeled,
   seeded and chopped
½ tsp. of oregano
2 to 3 envelopes of Sweet 'N Low
3 tbsps. of diced pimiento
4 tbsps. of wine vinegar

3 tbsps. of chopped parsley
½ cup of diced celery
1 tsp. of salt
⅛ tsp. of pepper
Sacramento Tomato Juice (optional)

Stew the eggplant in a Teflon pan with a little water or tomato juice for a few minutes. Remove the eggplant from the pan. Add onions and garlic to the pan and stew for a few minutes. Add tomatoes and simmer for 2 to 3 minutes; then, mix in eggplant, wine vinegar, and the parsley, oregano, celery, salt, pepper and sweetener. Simmer for several minutes. Stir in pimiento and chill for several hours. Serve 4-oz. portions for dinner.

NOTE: This may also be eaten hot.

"FRIED" EGGPLANT SLICES

1¼ lb. eggplant, peeled and sliced thin
½ cup of powdered skimmed milk
⅛ tsp. of garlic powder
⅛ tsp. of oregano
½ tsp. of salt
Sprinkles of pepper

Salt the eggplant slices for 15 to 20 minutes; wipe with paper towels. Dip the eggplant slices in dry mixture made from all of the other ingredients. (Dip both sides of the slices.) Place on a Teflon cookie sheet and bake for 5 minutes in a 350° pre-heated oven. With oven on the **same** temperature, place the pan in the broiler part of oven and broil until the top is nicely browned. Serves 4.

This is a limited dinner vegetable. After the eggplant is peeled, it should weigh about 1 lb. This dish can be re-heated.

Remember to count the milk toward your daily allowance.

GINGER CARROTS

Fresh carrots, sliced
Water
Salt, dried ginger and sweetener, to taste

Peel and slice the carrots on the diagonal. Cook in very little water, adding seasonings. This is a limited vegetable; serve a 4-oz. portion.

CANNED MARINATED VEGETABLES

1 small can of cut-up string beans
1 small can of peas and carrots
1 medium onion, sliced into thin rings
2 stalks of celery, cut diagonally in ¼″ slices
Salt, pepper, garlic powder and
    lemon juice, to taste

Mix all vegetables together and season lightly with spices. Squeeze the juice of ½ lemon over all and marinate in the refrigerator for 1 hour or more.

This is marvelous for a cook-out since it can be made several hours before needed. Remember . . . this is a limited vegetable and is to be served in 4-oz. portions at dinner.

MARINATED STRING BEANS

1-lb. can of cut-up string beans, drained

2 pimientos, cut up
3 sliced scallions
Good Seasons Low Calorie Italian Dressing,
    made up as directed on the package

Mix all of the above ingredients together and marinate the vegetables in the mixture for several hours.

SWEET BASIL PEAS

1 lb. of green peas
1/3 cup of water
1 small onion, finely diced
1 tsp. of salt
1 tsp. of sweet basil
1 clove of garlic, split in half
Sprinkles of pepper
½ envelope of Sweet 'N Low

Place the onion in water and simmer, covered, for a few minutes. Add the peas and all of the other ingredients and continue to cook, covered, until the peas are tender. Check the seasoning since you may want to add a little more salt. Serve 4-oz. portions for dinner only.

NOTE: If you wish to make this an unlimited vegetable, use french-cut string or waxed beans and substitute 1 tbsp. of onion flakes for the fresh onion.

BAKED MASHED FROZEN SQUASH

1 package of cooked squash (frozen)
Cinnamon, sweetener and nutmeg

Place defrosted squash in a Teflon pie plate, and sprinkle liberally with cinnamon and sweetener. Add several pinches of nutmeg. Bake, covered, in a 350° oven for 15 to 20 minutes. Since this is a limited vegetable, serve 4-oz. portions.

MOCK RATATOUILLE

1 eggplant, peeled and cubed
1 large or 2 medium zucchini
1 4-oz. can of mushrooms, and the liquid
2 medium, ripe tomatoes, peeled
  and chopped
4 tbsps. of wine vinegar
½ tsp. of oregano
1 envelope of Sweet 'N Low
½ cup diced onion
½ cup diced celery
2 cloves of garlic
3 tbsps. of chopped parsley
Salt and pepper, to taste

Stew the zucchini and eggplant in a Teflon pan, covered, with the mushroom liquid for a few minutes. Remove the vegetables from the pan. Now, stew the onions and garlic for a few minutes, add the tomatoes and simmer, covered, 4 to 5 minutes longer. Mix in the vegetables, wine vinegar, parsley, oregano, celery, salt, pepper and sweetener . . . including the mushrooms. Simmer, covered, until done (according to your preference). The vegetables should be slightly crisp. This tastes best served cold!

Serve 4-oz. portions for dinner only as this is a limited vegetable meal!

FRESH MUSHROOMS AND PEAS

½ lb. of fresh mushrooms,
   cleaned and sliced
½ to 1 envelope of MBT Chicken Broth
Sprinkles of pepper
¼ tsp. of salt, or more
1 pkg. of frozen peas, thawed
¼ cup of water
Pimiento

Place broth, mushrooms and water in a skillet and cook, uncovered, for several minutes. Add peas and seasonings and cook, uncovered, for several minutes longer. If too much liquid remains, cook down quickly on high flame. Garnish with diced pimiento.

This is a limited dinner vegetable and should be served in 4-oz. portions.

FRESH TOMATOES

Slice a 4-oz. tomato. Sprinkle the slices with salt, pepper, dill weed or oregano, to taste, and refrigerate for a few minutes until chilled.

VEGETABLE MEDLEY

1 pkg. of frozen artichokes
1 4-oz. can of mushrooms, and liquid
1 chopped green pepper
1 diced onion
6 ozs. of cooked-down tomato juice
Sprinkling of Parmesan cheese, salt,
   pepper and sweet basil

Stew the onion and pepper in tomato juice for 5 to 10 minutes until they start to soften. Add the artichokes, mushrooms and liquid, salt, pepper and sweet basil and cook, covered, until all of the vegetables are done. If there is too much liquid, cook down for a few minutes, uncovered. Add sprinkle of cheese, stir and serve.

Serve 4-oz. portions as this is a limited dinner vegetable.

IRISH VEGETABLES

½ large cabbage
½ lb. of carrots, whole
2 envelopes of MBT Beef Broth
½ tsp. of pickling spices
Salt, to taste
Water to cover vegetables

Simmer all of the above, mixed together, until the vegetables are tender. Since this is limited, serve 4-oz. carrot portions at dinner only. Cabbage is free; unlimited.

Salads and Dressings

Allow salads to play an important role in your diet plan. Certainly use leftovers for Salads. A cold Salad plate is a welcome dish in warm weather.

Try Chicken or Turkey Salad, Crabmeat or Shrimp Salad or Chef's Salad, and add some cold unlimited vegetables to complete your meal. You can always add 4 ozs. of cooked peas to your protein in making up your salad.

If your preference is for gelatin salads, by all means try the Molded Fruit Ring with cottage cheese for a refreshing luncheon dish. Or, serve it for dessert following a cold salad.

Try the various Salad Dressings. Add one teaspoon of freeze-dried chives to any of the dressings in this section for a pleasant change. For an unusual dressing for salad greens, toss with Sesame-Poppy Seed Dressing . . and enjoy!

CHEF'S SALAD

6 ozs. of cooked chicken, veal, turkey,
　shellfish or other cold fish
Lettuce—head, romaine, or other greens,
　or a combination

½ cucumber, scored and sliced thin
4 ozs. tomato, cut up
Asparagus spears
½ diced red or green pepper

Using a large salad bowl, break up the greens after they have been washed and dried. Score the cucumber with a fork and slice thin. Arrange the slices around the outside of your bowl. Line asparagus spears, drained, around the inside of the cucumber slices. Place diced chicken, turkey or other protein in the center. Top with tomato slices or wedges and diced peppers. Refrigerate for 10 to 15 minutes, or longer. Add Tomato-Buttermilk or Mediterranean Dressing (pp. 144-145).

NOTE: This can be used for lunch by eliminating tomato and using 4 ozs. of protein . . . possibly 2 hard-boiled eggs cut into wedges. The recipe will serve 1 for dinner.

CHICKEN OR TURKEY SALAD

32 ozs. of boiled chicken or turkey, cold
1½ cups of diced celery
Salt and pepper to taste
1 cup of Good Seasons Low-Calorie
    Italian Salad Dressing, made up with
    water and wine vinegar (refer to
    directions on the package)
1-⅔ tbsps. of prepared mustard
1 pimiento, diced (optional)
1 tbsp. of sesame seeds, toasted (optional)

Combine the mustard and salad dressing and mix with all other ingredients. Refrigerate for one hour or more.

This recipe will serve 8 for lunch; 5 for dinner.

NOTE: This is marvelous as a dinner meal if you add 4 ozs. of cooked, frozen peas (per serving) as your #4 vegetable (limited).

For making an individual portion (dinner for one), the ingredients are as follows:

6 ozs. of cooked, diced chicken or turkey
4 ozs. of cooked, frozen peas
¼ cup of diced celery
Salt and pepper, to taste
1 tsp. of prepared mustard
3 tbsps. of Good Seasons Low-Calorie
   Italian Salad Dressing, made up with
   water and wine vinegar (refer to
   directions on the package)
Diced pimiento (optional)
1 tsp. sesame seeds, toasted

CRABMEAT OR SHRIMP SALAD

4 ozs. of crabmeat or shrimp
Lettuce leaves
Seafood Cocktail Sauce (p. 147)
Lemon wedges

Arrange lettuce leaves on a dish. Place the seafood around the outer edge of the plate. Fill the center with Seafood Cocktail Sauce. Serve with lemon wedges.

This recipe will serve 1 for lunch. For dinner, increase the shell fish to 6-oz. portion.

FRUIT-VEGETABLE SALAD

½ orange, peeled and sliced thin
3 ozs. of tomato, sliced
1 oz. of onion, sliced and
   separated into rings
Lettuce leaf
French-Type or Tomato Buttermilk Dressing (p. 144)

Place the orange slices on top of a large lettuce leaf. Top with tomato slices and onion rings. Chill. Serve with desired dressing.

This is a salad that may be used at dinner only as the tomato and onion are limited dinner vegetables. Count the orange as half of daily citrus fruit.

MOLDED FRUIT RING

Gelatin
2 pkgs. of Unsweetened Strawberry
   Cheeri-Aid or Kool-Aid
4 envelopes of unflavored Knox Gelatin
3 cups of cold water
3 cups of boiling water
4 tbsps. of Sweet 'N Low
2 ozs. of lemon juice (optional)

Make your gelatin mixture by softening the Knox Gelatin in cold water; then, add boiling water to dissolve the gelatin. Add Cheeri-Aid (or Kool-Aid), sweetener and lemon juice. Chill to consistency of jelly.

Fruit
1 lb. of rhubarb, cut up

½ pineapple, diced
8 strawberries
2 ozs. of water
5 envelopes of Sweet 'N Low

Cut up the rhubarb and dice the pineapple fine. Cook the rhubarb, water, pineapple and strawberries in a covered saucepan until the fruit is soft. (Strawberries and rhubarb will be completely cooked; the pineapple may be a little firm.) Add sweetener.

When the gelatin mixture is syrupy, add the fruit mixture and place in a mold. Refrigerate until set—preferably overnight. Serves 8 to 10.

This mold contains three fruits. Up to 4 ozs. of rhubarb is unlimited.

NOTE: The recipe is given in large amounts since it will stay in the refrigerator for at least four or five days. It's so good that even non-dieters will enjoy it!

"LEGAL" GELATIN MOLD

1 pkg. of unsweetened Cheeri-Aid or
    unsweetened Kool-Aid
2 envelopes of unflavored Knox Gelatin
2 tbsps. of Sweet 'N Low
1½ cups of cold water
1½ cups of boiling water
Juice of ¼ to ½ lemon, or
    1 oz. ReaLemon

Soften the Cheeri-Aid (or Kool-Aid) and gelatin in cold water. Add boiling water to dissolve. Add the sweetener and lemon juice, and stir well. Refrigerate until set.

This mold is unlimited at any time of day.

SESAME-POPPY SEED DRESSING

4 ozs. of tomato juice
4 ozs. of buttermilk
¾ tsp. of poppy seeds
1 tsp. of sesame seeds, **toasted**
½ tsp. of salt
1 tsp. dried onion flakes
⅛ tsp. of oregano
Sprinkles of garlic powder, dill weed
   and pepper
½ tsp. of unflavored Knox Gelatin
½ envelope of Sweet 'N Low

Soften the gelatin in tomato juice. Bring to a boil to dissolve the gelatin. Allow to cool. Add all of the other ingredients and refrigerate.

NOTE: Remember to count the tomato juice and buttermilk used toward your daily allowance. This will stay well in the refrigerator for two or three days at least!

WINE VINEGAR DRESSING

2 ozs. of Heinz Wine Vinegar
1 oz. of water
5 ozs. of tomato juice
1 envelope of Sweet 'N Low
Garlic powder, salt and pepper

Mix all ingredients together and refrigerate. Count the tomato juice toward your daily allowance!

ITALIAN-STYLE DRESSING

12 ozs. of tomato juice
2 ozs. of wine vinegar
1 tsp. of lemon juice
1 tsp. of dried onion flakes
1 tsp. of dry mustard
Salt, to taste
1 tsp. of KikkoMan Soy Sauce
Several shakes of garlic powder
¼ tsp. of rosemary
¼ to ½ tsp. of sweet basil
Sweetener, to taste

Mix all of the above ingredients together and let stand for a short while. Put the mixture into a blender and run for 30 seconds. Refrigerate. This will serve 6.

Variation: Use 6 ozs. of tomato juice and 6 ozs. of buttermilk instead of 12 ozs. of tomato juice. Count the tomato juice and buttermilk toward your daily allowance!

BLENDER FRENCH DRESSING

1 cup of tomato juice
4 tbsps. of wine vinegar
4 tbsps. of finely chopped green pepper
1 tsp. of Worcestershire Sauce
1 tsp. of salt
1 tsp. of dry mustard
1 clove of garlic, or garlic powder
to taste
1 envelope of Sweet 'N Low
2 tsps. dried onion flakes

Place all of the ingredients in a blender and run for a minute on "low." Refrigerate. This recipe will serve 6.

NOTE: Count the tomato juice as part of your daily allowance.

TOMATO-BUTTERMILK DRESSING

⅔ cup of tomato juice
⅔ cup of buttermilk
1 tsp. dried onion flakes
2 ozs. more of tomato juice
1 tsp. of unflavored Knox Gelatin
½ tsp. of McCormick's Season-All powder
Garlic powder, salt and pepper, to taste
½ envelope of Sweet 'N Low

Soften 1 tsp. of gelatin in 2 ozs. of tomato juice. Bring to a boil and then allow to cool. Add the other ingreidents and refrigerate. This will thicken.

NOTE: Count the tomato juice and buttermilk as part of your daily allowances!

FRENCH-TYPE DRESSING

1 cup of tomato juice
4 tbsps. of lemon juice or wine vinegar
1 tbsp. dried onion flakes
Salt and pepper, to taste
1 clove of garlic, split,
   or ⅛ tsp. of garlic powder
Few pinches of oregano
1 envelope of Sweet 'N Low

Combine all of the above ingredients in a jar and refrigerate. Shake well before using.

Count the tomato juice toward your daily allowance. If you use buttermilk, remember to count that toward your daily milk allowance.

Variation: Use ½ tomato juice and ½ buttermilk instead of 1 cup of tomato juice.

MEDITERRANEAN DRESSING

1 pkg. of Good Seasons Low-Calorie
   Italian Salad Dressing Mix
2 ozs. of lemon juice
2 tbsps. of water
⅔ cup of buttermilk
1 clove of garlic
⅛ tsp. of oregano

Mix the lemon juice and water together. Add the salad dressing and garlic clove and shake well. Add buttermilk and oregano, and shake again. This will serve 6.

Count the buttermilk and/or tomato juice toward your daily allowances.

Variation: This can be changed by using half buttermilk and half tomato juice, 1 tsp. dried onion flakes and a little sweetener, to taste.

"MAYONNAISE" MUSTARD DRESSING

2 tsps. of powdered skimmed milk
1 tbsp. of water
1½ tsps. of mild prepared mustard
1 tsp. dried onion flakes (optional)
Salt and pepper (light)

Mix milk and water together; then, add the other ingredients. This is excellent to moisten **cold leftover** fish or mashed hard-boiled eggs. This can also be used with cold tuna and salmon to which diced celery can be added.

NOTE: For egg salad, a sprinkle of celery seed can be added; and with fish, you might wish to add dill.

Sauces and Relishes

Sauces for leftovers can be a boon as well as a way to make tasty meals since they are so simple to make. If you have time to prepare your sauce for fish, eggs, chicken, etc. in advance, do so by all means. The flavor of the sauce will improve, and thicken, if allowed to refrigerate for a half hour or more.

The Barbecue Sauces are adaptable and can be used with poultry, veal or fish. They may be frozen, for your convenience.

If you are a catsup or chili sauce lover, do try the recipes that follow. You can keep them indefinitely!

A word for Seafood Cocktail Sauce! Use it with shrimp, crab, lobster, and even to "dunk" an artichoke!

SEAFOOD COCKTAIL SAUCE

2 cups of tomato juice, cooked down (p. 9)
2 tbsps. of white horseradish
3 tbsps. of lemon juice
2 tbsps. of Worcestershire Sauce
2 envelopes of Sweet 'N Low

Simmer a 46-oz. can of tomato juice, uncovered, for 1½ to 2 hours to yield 2 or 2½ cups (quite thick). Cool.

Then add other ingredients mentioned and refrigerate.
This will stay for weeks in the refrigerator.

Remember to count tomato juice as part of your
daily allowance.

This is luscious with shellfish or cold, leftover fish.
It's also very good for dipping artichoke leaves.

SAUCE FOR LEFTOVERS #1

4 ozs. of buttermilk
¼ cucumber (diced fine)
1 tsp. of dried onion flakes,
   or freeze-dried chives
McCormick's Season-All powder, to taste
Several sprinkles of dill weed
½ to 1 tsp. of drained capers
2 tbsps. of diced celery (optional)
Salt and pepper to taste
Sweetener, to taste
Garlic powder (optional)

Mix all of the ingredients together and allow to refrigerate for at least 10 to 20 minutes for the flavors to
blend. Use this with cold, leftover fish which has been
broken into chunks or flaked . . . or use it with chicken
or turkey. This will stay in the refrigerator for several
days.

This is ¼ of your daily milk allowance.

SAUCE FOR LEFTOVERS #2

2 ozs. of buttermilk
1 tsp. of dried onion flakes (optional)
½ tsp. of mild prepared mustard

1½ tsps. of drained capers
1 tsp. of Green Pickle Relish (p. 152)
Salt and pepper, to taste
Dash of sweetener

Mix all of the ingredients together and allow to stand for a few minutes. Add to tuna, salmon, cold fish or hard-boiled eggs.

Remember to count the buttermilk toward your daily allowance.

SAUCE FOR COLD FISH

6 ozs. of cooked-down tomato juice
1 tsp. of white vinegar
⅛ tsp. of pumpkin pie spice
¼ tsp. of Sweet 'N Low
6 ozs. of buttermilk
1 tsp. dried onion flakes

Mix the tomato juice with vinegar, pumpkin pie spice and sweetener. This should taste like chili sauce. Add buttermilk and onion flakes to the mixture and chill well. Serve over cold leftover fish or shellfish!

Count the tomato juice and buttermilk toward your daily allowances.

BARBECUE SAUCE #1

¾ cup of chopped onion
⅓ cup of wine vinegar
2½ cups of cooked-down tomato juice
  (reduced from 5 cups)
⅓ cup of lemon juice

3 tbsps. of prepared mustard
3 tbsps. of Worcestershire Sauce
1½ tsps. of salt
¼ to ½ tsps. of pepper
3 envelopes of Sweet 'N Low

Mix all of the mentioned ingredients together, and refrigerate. This sauce can stay in the refrigerator for several days and can also be frozen.

Remember to count the tomato juice and onion toward your daily allowances. Serve this at dinner only.

BARBECUE SAUCE #2

1 qt. of tomato juice
1 green pepper, diced
2 tbsps. of dried onion flakes
1 tbsp. of prepared mustard
2 tbsps. of Worcestershire Sauce
¼ tsp. of garlic powder
3 ozs. of wine vinegar
½ tsp. of salt
⅛ tsp. of pepper
1 envelope of Sweet 'N Low

Simmer all of the ingredients together except the sweetener in an uncovered saucepan for about 1 hour. The sauce should be quite thick. Add the sweetener after the sauce has finished cooking. This sauce freezes very well. Can be served at lunch or dinner.

Remember to count the tomato juice toward your daily allowance. You can use this sauce over chicken, fish or veal.

"LEGAL" CHILI SAUCE

12 ozs. of tomato juice,
    cooked down to 6 ozs.
1 tsp. of white vinegar
⅛ to ¼ tsp. of allspice
    or pumpkin pie spice
¼ to ½ tsp. of Sweet 'N Low

Mix all of the above together and allow to chill. It's great on cold fish or mixed with cold flaked fish.

My preference is for the pumpkin pie spice in making up the sauce. Remember to count the tomato juice toward your daily allowance.

DIETER'S CATSUP

4 cups of tomato juice
4 tbsps. of distilled white vinegar
½ tsp. of allspice
2 tsps. of dried mustard
1 onion, cut in half
2 to 3 envelopes of Sweet 'N Low

Place the tomato juice, vinegar, alspice, mustard and onion in a saucepan and bring to a boil. Allow to simmer until quite thick (about 1 to 2 hours). Allow to cool. Remove the onion and add sweetener. Refrigerate. This can stay refrigerated indefinitely. This recipe makes up about one-half of a bottle of catsup. Use sparingly as the tomato juice should be counted daily.

LAZY DIETER'S CATSUP

16 ozs. of tomato juice
4 capsful of KikkoMan Soy Sauce
Sweet 'N Low, to taste

Simmer juice and soy sauce over a low flame, for about 2 hours. Allow to cool, and then add sweetener to taste. Refrigerate.

Use sparingly, or count the tomato juice toward your daily allowance.

GREEN PICKLE RELISH

1 dill pickle, cut up
1 tsp. of white vinegar
1 envelope of Sweet 'N Low

Blend all of the above ingredients on "low" speed until mixture is of the desired consistency. This will stay well in the refrigerator. It's marvelous on frankfurters or hamburgers. This is unlimited so enjoy it!

NOTE: If the flavor is too strong, add 1 tbsp. of water.

Breads and Stuffings

Zwieback can be made and kept for many days . . . and it's a welcome change from a slice of toast. Make up four slices or more at a time and wrap them in a plastic bag.

If you are a dessert lover, consider making the Pie Crust for lunch with one of the pudding fillings found in the Fruits and Desserts section! Try the Veal Pie for luncheon only (p. 57).

When using poultry, try a little stuffing! For lunch it can be Mushroom-Bread Stuffing; for dinner, try the Vegetable Stuffing (it's unlimited).

ZWIEBACK

4 slices of white enriched bread
Cinnamon and sweetener mixture (p. 10)

Sprinkle the cinnamon and sweetener mixture liberally on one side of the white bread. Place the bread in a 200° oven for about 20 minutes. Turn the bread over and sprinkle the cinnamon and sweetener mixture on the other side. Bake for another 20 minutes, until the bread is all dried out. This will serve 4.

PIE CRUST

2 slices of white bread (enriched),
   baked at 350° for 10 minutes;
   then blended into crumbs
1 tsp. of vanilla
1 tbsp. of dry powdered skimmed milk
1 tbsp. of water
1 to 2 envelopes of Sweet 'N Low

This is for a small Teflon loaf pan. Mix the dry
ingredients together first; then, add the water and
vanilla. Use your fingers—it's easier! Pat the mixture
into the bottom of the pan and bake at 350° for 8 to 10
minutes. Allow to cool before filling. This will serve 2!

MUSHROOM-BREAD STUFFING

2 slices of enriched white bread, toasted
1½ tbsps. dried onion flakes
1 envelope MBT Chicken Broth
2 ozs. of canned mushrooms and
   2 ozs. of mushroom liquid
2 ozs. of water
¼ cup of celery, diced fine
½ tsp. of parsley flakes
¼ tsp. of poultry seasoning
¼ tsp. of salt
Sprinkles of garlic powder and pepper

Dice the bread into croutons. Bring mushroom liquid and 2 ozs. of water to a boil and dissolve the broth.
Add all of the other ingredients, mix together, and stuff
your poultry. You may bake the stuffing separately in a

Teflon junior loaf pan, if desired. If baking separately, bake uncovered at 350° for 40 to 50 minutes. If you prefer to stuff half of a 3-lb. broiler-fryer for lunch for two, make a circle of stuffing in a small roasting pan and place the chicken, skin-side up, on top. Season the chicken with garlic powder, salt, pepper and paprika. Bake at 350°, covered, for 30 minutes; then, uncover and bake for 30 or more minutes longer. Serve at lunch only.

VEGETABLE STUFFING

1 pkg. of cauliflower, frozen
4 ozs. of water
1 envelope MBT Chicken Broth
2 ozs. of canned mushrooms, drained
1 tbsp. of dried onion flakes
1 tbsp. of chopped parsley
Sprinkles of garlic powder
Sprinkles of pepper
¼ to ½ tsp. of poultry seasoning
Paprika

Cook the cauliflower in ½ package of broth and 4 ozs. of water until the cauliflower is soft, but not mushy. Remove from the liquid and chop or cut into small pieces. Add the mushrooms which have been diced, dried onion flakes, parsley, ½ envelope of broth, pepper, garlic powder and poultry seasoning. Mix all together. Stuff the cavity of a chicken or turkey, or bake in a Teflon loaf pan (at 350° for 30 minutes, uncovered).

Jellies and Conserves

Even if you have never liked cranberries, don't miss the Cranberry Conserve in this section! It's so easy to make . . . so good on toast . . . and freezable, too!

Buy up cranberries when they're in season and freeze them in the original cartons so that you can enjoy this all year long!

Strawberry jelly can be available all year now that frozen whole strawberries (without sugar, of course) are in the Frozen Food Section of your market. Jelly can be frozen, if desired.

STRAWBERRY OR BLUEBERRY JELLY

16 strawberries, fresh or frozen,
    or 1 cup blueberries
Little water
1 to 2 envelopes of Sweet 'N Low
Lemon juice (optional)

Cook berries, covered, in a little water until the consistency of jelly. If you like your jelly thicker, soften 1 tsp. of unflavored Knox Gelatin in 1 oz. of cold water; then, add to the hot berry mixture. Add sweetener and lemon juice, if desired.

If taken on dry toast in the morning in 1 tsp. servings, this need not be counted in your daily allowance. Each jelly contains two fruits . . . so beware!

Variations: You can use two peaches, ½ of a pineapple, etc., for the fruit.

RHUBARB CONSERVE

1 lb. fresh rhubarb, washed and cut up
8 strawberries
2 ozs. of water
1 tsp. of unflavored Knox Gelatin
   and 1 oz. of water
Several strips of lemon peel
3 to 4 envelopes of Sweet 'N Low

Simmer rhubarb, strawberries and lemon peel in a covered saucepan until rhubarb is soft. Stir once in a while while cooking. Soften gelatin in 1 oz. of cold water; then, add to the hot rhubarb mixture. Sweeten to taste, and refrigerate. (4 ozs. of rhubarb is considered unlimited. 8 strawberries are equal to one fruit! OVER 4 ozs. of rhubarb must be considered as one fruit; 4 ozs. or less is unlimited. Therefore, count 4 ozs. or more of rhubarb as one fruit per 4-oz. serving.)

If you are using frozen rhubarb, use 1¼ lb. package of rhubarb and 8 strawberries, but DO NOT add 2 ozs. of water. The frozen rhubarb gives off a great deal of liquid. This recipe is luscious on toast, or as an accompaniment to poultry.

CRANBERRY CONSERVE

1 box of cranberries
1 navel orange, diced fine (including the peel)
2 to 3 tbsps. of Sweet 'N Low
   (start with 2 tbsps.)
1 to 1½ cups of water

Cook the cranberries and diced orange in water gently, in a covered pot, for about ½ to ¾ of an hour, or until all of the cranberries have popped. Remove the cover and simmer until the cranberries are soft. You may have to add water. Add sweetener and refrigerate.

This stays well in the refrigerator for several weeks. It freezes well, also!

NOTE: This is marvelous on dry toast; use very sparingly. Remember—the one orange is a fruit.

Fruits and Desserts

If you are a dessert lover, these next pages are just for you! Perfect the Crustless Apple Pie and the Baked Apple Supreme and you have the start of a couple of really good desserts! Don't stop now! Try Peach or Strawberry Ice Cream . . . Pistachio, too! Or try any of the Puddings.

Freeze 4-oz. portions of evaporated skimmed milk in paper cups. Remove from the freezer when needed, peel off the paper cup, and you're almost ready to make your Ice Cream! Milk can stay frozen for several weeks.

In the summer, when peaches are inexpensive, buy them and freeze for use over the winter. Peel, slice and freeze peaches individually in Saran Wrap; then, place all peaches in a plastic bag and tie firmly. Peaches can stay frozen for months!

A word about the new artificial sweeteners. When cyclamates were taken off the market, it became increasingly difficult to sweeten foods as we were used to doing. However, please note that now the flavor of artificially sweetened foods change and improve after refrigeration. If you make a dish which should be served cold, don't add extra sweetener until after it has been chilled.

LEMON-LIME MELON PIE
Crust
4 slices of white enriched bread, baked
   at 250° for about 20 minutes
2 tsps. of vanilla
2 tbsps. of dry powdered milk
2 tbsps. of water
3 to 4 envelopes of Sweet 'N Low

Use the blender to make bread crumbs. Mix the dry ingredients together first. Add vanilla and water slowly and mix thoroughly. Press mixture into a Teflon pie plate and bake at 350° for 10 minutes, or until the crust is firm and has browned some.

Filling
½ cup of cold water
1 cup of boiling water
1 tbsp. of Lemon-Lime Cheeri-Aid,
   unsweetened
2 envelopes of unflavored Knox Gelatin
4 ozs. of evaporated skimmed milk
5 to 6 envelopes of Sweet 'N Low
½ cantaloupe, blended
½ cantaloupe, finely diced

Soften the gelatin in cold water. Add boiling water to dissolve the gelatin. Add Cheeri-Aid, sweetener, ½ of cantaloupe which has been blended, and then the 4 ozs. of evaporated skimmed milk. (If the milk is frozen, the dessert can be made very quickly.) Refrigerate until syrupy; then, add ½ diced cantaloupe. Pour into a pre-baked pie crust and refrigerate.

NOTE: Consider the milk toward your daily

allowance. The entire pie is two fruits, and will serve four for lunch only!

Variation: Use honeydew melon. For blended melon, use 1 cup of blended honeydew and then use 1 cup of diced honeydew for the diced fruit. This may not need as many as 5 to 6 envelopes of sweetener because honeydew melon can be sweeter than cantaloupe.

CRUSTLESS STRAWBERRY PIE #1

32 fresh or frozen strawberries
4 ozs. of water
2 envelopes of unflavored Knox Gelatin
4 ozs. of evaporated skimmed milk
2 ozs. of reconstituted lemon juice (ReaLemon)
6 to 7 envelopes of Sweet 'N Low

Bring the berries to a boil in 4 ozs. of water and then simmer for a minute or two. Soften the gelatin in the 2 ozs. of lemon juice and add this, with the sweetener, to the hot berry mixture. Allow to cool slightly before adding the evaporated skimmed milk. Pour the mixture into a pie plate and refrigerate. This does not take very long to set.

The pie can remain in your refrigerator for several days . . . and will serve 4.   Remember to count each portion as 1 fruit, and consider 1 oz. of evaporated skimmed milk toward your daily milk allowance.

CRUSTLESS STRAWBERRY PIE #2

1 envelope of unflavored Knox Gelatin
2 ozs. of cold water

4 ozs. of boiling water
2 to 3 envelopes of Sweet 'N Low
16 frozen or fresh strawberries
8 ozs. of buttermilk

Soften the gelatin in cold water; then, add the boiling water to dissolve. Place in a blender and add all of the other ingredients except 8 strawberries. Blend for a minute. Place in a Teflon pie plate and refrigerate. This can be used as a pudding by pouring into dessert dishes before refrigerating. Garnish the pie with 8 sliced strawberries.

Count this as ½ fruit and 2 ozs. of daily milk allowance. This pie will serve 4.

"ALMOST INSTANT" PEACH CHIFFON PIE

2 ripe, fresh peaches, peeled, pitted,
   sliced and frozen
8 ozs. of evaporated skimmed milk
1 envelope and 1 tsp. of unflavored
   Knox Gelatin
2 ozs. of cold water
4 ozs. of boiling water
4 drops of yellow food coloring
4 envelopes of Sweet 'N Low

Soften the gelatin in cold water for a few minutes. Add boiling water and stir until well dissolved. Add all of the other ingredients and place the mixture in a blender. Whirl until smooth. Pour into Teflon pie plate and refrigerate until set. If you wish, you can garnish with peach slices or mint leaves.

NOTE: Because the peaches are frozen and broken up some, when they are placed in a blender the result is a thickened mixture.

This recipe contains your entire daily milk allowance and two fruits, if the whole pie is eaten. If ¼ of the pie is eaten, count ¼ of your daily milk allowance and ½ of a fruit.

PINEAPPLE CHEESE CAKE

Crust
4 slices of white enriched bread
2 tsps. of vanilla
2 tbsps. of powdered skimmed milk
4 envelopes of Sweet 'N Low
2 tbsps. of water

Bake the bread at 250° for about 20 minutes, until dried out. Put each slice of bread separately in a blender. Run on "low" speed until fine crumbs are made. Mix the dry ingredients together first; then, add the vanilla and water slowly and mix thoroughly. Press mixture into a Teflon pie plate and bake at 350° for 10 minutes, or until crust is firm. Allow to cool.

Filling
½ of a very ripe pineapple, diced fine
2 envelopes of Sweet 'N Low
8 ozs. of water
8 ozs. of farmer cheese
1 pkg. of unflavored Knox Gelatin
4 ozs. of cold water
4 ozs. of boiling water

5 envelopes of Sweet 'N Low
4 to 5 drops of yellow food coloring

Cook the pineapple, diced fine, in 1 cup of water for about 1 hour, until the pineapple is very tender. Add more water, if needed. When you are finished, there should be no water left. Place the pineapple in the blender with 2 envelopes of Sweet 'N Low and run on "low" speed until the pineapple is of the consistency of puree. Soften the gelatin in 4 ozs. of cold water; then add the boiling water. Place in the blender with pineapple, farmer cheese, 5 envelopes of sweetener and 4 to 5 drops of yellow food coloring. Put the blender on "low" speed for a minute; then raise it to "high" speed for a minute. The mixture should be smooth and creamy. Pour into a baked pie crust and refrigerate for at least 1 hour.

NOTE: This can be used for lunch, but you will need to supplement the meal with 2 ozs. of farmer cheese. Count the milk and fruit for breakfast and lunch as follows: ½ tbsp. of powdered milk and ½ fruit per ¼ of the pie. Serves 4.

CRUSTLESS APPLE PIE

4 Rome Beauty apples, peeled and sliced
Cinnamon and sweetener mixture (p. 10)
2 pkgs. of unflavored Knox Gelatin
4 ozs. of water
2 ozs. of reconstituted lemon juice
   (ReaLemon)
2 envelopes of Sweet 'N Low
⅓ cup of dry powdered milk

Toss the apple slices with the cinnamon and sweetener mixture and place in a pie plate. (For better flavor, slice each apple separately, sprinkle with 1 tbsp. of cinnamon and sweetener mixture.) Soften the gelatin in lemon juice and water, and then bring it to a boil. Add the 2 envelopes of sweetener and pour over the apple slices. Re-sprinkle with cinnamon and sweetener mixture, if you wish. Sprinkle the dry powdered milk on top of the pie. Bake at 325° if your pie plate is glass; 350° if your using either Teflon or metal . . . for about 30 minutes. Remove pie from the oven, tilt the pan, and spoon the liquid over top of the pie to moisten the milk on top. Return to the oven and bake for approximately another 30 minutes. Refrigerate until the liquid has set, possibly several hours. Serves 4.

NOTE: Each portion is 1 fruit. Consider milk as part of your daily allowance.

STRAWBERRY BAVARIAN

1 tsp. of lemon juice
1 envelope of unflavored Knox Gelatin
¾ cup of cold water
¾ cup of boiling water
12 whole frozen strawberries
2 ozs. of evaporated skimmed milk,
    frozen in ice tray
6 envelopes of Sweet 'N Low

Soften the gelatin in cold water; then, dissolve in the boiling water. Allow to sit for a few minutes; then, add the sweetener and lemon juice. Place this in a blender and whirl with the frozen strawberries and frozen milk, until smooth. Pour into sherbet glasses or a pie plate, and refrigerate. You can also pour this into a Pie Crust (p. 154). The pie will serve 4.

The entire pie contains 1½ fruits and 2 ozs. of evaporated skimmed milk which are to be counted toward your daily allowances. If you use the Pie Crust, this may be eaten for lunch only.

CARROT-APPLE COOKIE

4 ozs. of grated carrots
1 Rome Beauty apple, including the peel
⅓ cup of powdered skimmed milk crystals
1 tbsp. of cinnamon and sweetener mixture (p. 10)

Grate the carrots and apple on the second largest side of a 4-sided grater, and add the dry milk and cinnamon-sweetener mixture. Drop mixture on a Teflon cookie sheet by tbsp. and flatten. Bake for 20 minutes at 350°. Use a Teflon pancake turner to turn and flatten cookies. Return cookies to the oven and bake 15 minutes longer. Turn cookies over once more and reduce oven heat to 200°. Bake until cookies are dried out and like chewy dried fruit. Continue to turn. (Do not cover tightly when storing; the cookies will become soft.) If the cookies **should** soften, just return them to the oven to dry out.

This is **only** to be used with your dinner meal because of the 4 ozs. of limited vegetable. Count 1 fruit, ½ of your daily milk allowance, and 4 ozs. of limited vegetable.

Variation: You may omit the carrots and use 1 cap of vanilla instead. The instructions remain the same.

PINEAPPLE PUDDING

1 cup of skimmed milk
4 ozs. of evaporated skimmed milk
3 envelopes of Sweet 'N Low
1½ tsps. of unflavored Knox Gelatin
1 tsp. of pineapple extract
4 drops of yellow food coloring

Soften the gelatin in mixture made of both of the milks. Place in saucepan and bring to a boil. Allow to stand for a few minutes. Add all of the other ingredients and chill in your refrigerator until consistency of syrup. Beat at "high" speed (in pre-chilled metal bowl and beaters) with electric mixer until the mixture is fluffy and doubled in volume . . . about 5 minutes. Spoon into dessert dishes and refrigerate. Garnish with fresh sliced strawberries. This stays nicely in the refrigerator overnight. Serves 3 to 4.

NOTE: This is the equivalent to a whole day's milk allowance. Also, remember to count the strawberries toward part of your daily fruit allowance.

FLUFFY PINEAPPLE PUDDING

2 tsps. of unflavored Knox Gelatin
2 cups of liquified skimmed milk
1 tsp. of Wagner Pineapple Flavor,
   or other pineapple extract
3 envelopes of Sweet 'N Low
4 drops of yellow food coloring
Strawberries to garnish (optional)

Sprinkle the gelatin over the skimmed milk in a

saucepan. Cook over low heat until the gelatin is dissolved (almost to a boil). Allow to stand for a few minutes before adding the extract, sweetener and food coloring. Chill in the refrigerator until the mixture is syrupy. Using the electric mixer (remember the pre-chilled metal bowl and beaters), beat at high speed until the mixture is fluffy and doubled in volume. Spoon into dessert dishes and chill until set. Garnish with sliced strawberries (optional . . . but so pretty).

This will stay well in the refrigerator for a day or two. It's luscious, light and tasty, and is excellent after a heavy meal. Serves 4.

NOTE: Count each serving as 4 ozs. of daily milk allowance. You can eat this any time of day.

Be adventurous! Try other flavored extracts for variety.

BUTTERSCOTCH INSTANT PUDDING

1½ envelopes of unflavored Knox Gelatin
2 ozs. of cold water
2 ozs. of boiling water
4 ozs. of evaporated skimmed milk
2 caps of butterscotch extract
½ cap of vanilla extract
5 envelopes of Sweet 'N Low
8 crushed ice cubes
5 drops of yellow food coloring

Soften the gelatin in cold water; then add the boiling water to dissolve the gelatin. Add evaporated skimmed milk and all of the other ingredients, except the crushed ice. Place the mixture in a blender with ½ of the crushed ice. Blend, and then add the balance of the ice. The pudding can be eaten now and does not need any further refrigeration. Serves 4.

The recipe can be varied by changing the extracts and the food coloring. Remember to count the milk toward your daily allowance.

SPICY PEACHES

1 peach, peeled and sliced
    (or try a nectarine)
½ cup of black cherry diet soda
2 whole cloves

Cook the peach slices in diet soda for a few minutes. Take the slices out and add cloves to the liquid. Cook down, uncovered, until a few tablespoons remain. Remove the cloves and spoon the liquid over peach slices. Chill.

Remember to count this as one fruit!

BAKED APPLE SUPREME

8 to 10 Rome Beauty apples
1 qt. of Cott's Black Cherry Diet Soda
1 orange, sliced **paper thin**
1 lemon, sliced **paper thin**
Cinnamon and sweetener mixture (p. 10)
8 to 10 whole cloves
Dried lemon and orange peel (optional)

Core the apples half way through, and with a potato peeler, peel 1 inch around the cored top. Arrange the apples, cut-side down, in a large roasting pan and pour soda over the apples. Bake uncovered at 350° for 15 minutes or longer. Turn the apples over and spoon some of the soda into the cavity of each apple. Sprinkle tops of apples generously with the cinnamon and sweetener mixture and top with a slice of orange; then a slice of lemon. Push 1 whole clove into the center of the lemon slice. Re-sprinkle with cinnamon and sweetener mixture. Sprinkle with dried lemon peel and dried orange peel (optional). Return to the oven and continue baking, uncovered, at 350° for at least 1 to 1¼ hours, or until the apples feel soft to the touch.

Remove the pan from the oven and take off lemon and orange slices. Set aside. Turn the apples over again, cut-side down, and allow to cool for at least an hour. Turn apples right side up, replace the fruit slices and cloves, and pour the liquid from the pan over all. Refrigerate until well chilled. This recipe freezes very well!

NOTE: While this sounds complicated (it may take you a few minutes extra the first time this recipe is made), the effort is worth it! You'll hear nothing but raves!

If you really want to make your apples even more elegant, spoon Cranberry Conserve (p. 158) into the apple cavities instead of using the diet soda. Then follow the recipe as given.

If you should use the Cranberry Conserve and fruit slices, count each apple as 1¼ fruits.

APPLE CASSEROLE

1 small apple, cored and sliced thin
2 tbsps. of orange juice
Cinnamon and sweetener mixture (p. 10)

Arrange in a small baking dish. Pour orange juice over the apples and add a few sprinkles of nutmeg. Bake uncovered in a pre-heated 350° oven until the apple slices are soft and tops brown.

This counts as one fruit since you will be using a small apple rather than the medium apple which you usually are allowed. The 2 tbsps. of juice, together with the small apple, equal one fruit!

RAW APPLE SLICE RING

1 red Delicious apple
Lemon juice
Cinnamon and sweetener mixture (p. 10)
  to taste

Leave skin on the apple, cut core and slice thin. Separate the slices on a dish, making a circle of slices. Sprinkle lightly with lemon juice. Then, spread the cinnamon and sweetener mixture on top . . . and enjoy!

This, of course, counts as one fruit.

This section on making ice cream will be much easier for you if you remember to keep your stainless steel mixing bowl and beaters in your freezer at all times. You'll always know where they are, and they will be chilled and always ready for use (p. 11).

PEACH OR STRAWBERRY ICE CREAM

4 ozs. of evaporated skimmed milk
8 frozen strawberries, or 1 sliced frozen peach
3 envelopes of Sweet 'N Low

Several drops of vanilla (optional)
Several drops of food coloring
    (yellow for peaches; red for
    strawberries, if desired)

Freeze the milk in a paper cup (it should be in a solid frozen state). Ten to 15 minutes before making the ice cream, remove the milk and fruit from your freezer and allow to stand at room temperature. Then, cut up the milk and fruit into chunks, and with your mixer on low speed, mix until smooth. Raise the mixer to a higher speed until you have the desired consistency. Place in the freezer for 10 minutes before eating, if desired.

This is a generous portion and very enjoyable! It takes a very short time to make this up and is a delicious dessert. This is best made fresh each time you want it.

NOTE: This counts as ½ of your daily milk allowance and one fruit, if you are eating the entire amount.

PINEAPPLE ICE CREAM

¼ of a medium pineapple, very ripe
4 ozs. of evaporated skimmed milk, frozen
2 envelopes of Sweet 'N Low

Cut the pineapple into small pieces and place in the blender for a few seconds only. Place in aluminum foil (make a flat packet) and store in your freezer. When ready to make up the ice cream, remove the frozen milk and frozen pineapple from the freezer and allow to stay at room temperature for 5 to 10 minutes, depending on warmth and humidity.

Chop up the milk and fruit and place in your chilled stainless steel bowl. With mixer on low speed, mix until there are no lumps. Raise the speed to high and beat until double in volume. If you're doing this on a humid day, return ice cream to the freezer for about 10 minutes before eating. This should be the consistency of store-bought ice cream.

Count this as ½ of your daily milk allowance and 1 fruit.

PISTACHIO ICE CREAM

4 ozs. of evaporated skimmed milk,
   frozen
1 peach, peeled, diced and frozen
2 to 3 envelopes of Sweet 'N Low
½ cap of vanilla
½ cap of almond extract
Several drops of green food coloring

Partially thaw the milk and peach. Chop up into chunks with a knife and place in a pre-chilled metal bowl. Add the extracts, sweetener and food coloring. On low speed, mix all of the ingredients until smooth. Raise speed to high and beat until the volume is doubled. Place in the freezer until firm (just a few minutes).

This recipe will serve 2. Each serving equals ½ fruit and ¼ of your daily milk allowance.

NOTE: Weather is important here. If you're making this on a warm, humid day, this may not be as firm as it should be. In this case, re-freeze it!

FRUITLESS PISTACHIO ICE CREAM

4 ozs. of evaporated skimmed milk, frozen
½ cap of vanilla extract
½ cap of almond extract
2 envelopes of Sweet 'N Low
2 drops of green food coloring

Defrost the milk about 5 to 10 minutes. Chop up.
Place the milk in a pre-chilled metal bowl and add extracts, sweetener and food coloring. Using pre-chilled
beaters and with the mixer on low speed, mix until
smooth. Raise mixer to high speed and mix until
double in volume. Return to the freezer until the
desired consistency.

Again, the weather is important. If you're making
this on a warm, humid day this may not be as firm as it
should be. In this case, re-freeze it!

This recipe serves 2, and is ¼ of the daily milk
allowance.

SOFT FRESH FRUIT ICE CREAM

1 peach, pitted, peeled and sliced,
   or 8 frozen or fresh strawberries
¼ cup of water
⅓ cup of dry skimmed milk powder
10 ice cubes, crushed
3 envelopes of Sweet 'N Low, or more

Place the water in a blender first, with the fruit, and
blend until pureed. Add the sweetener, powdered milk
and crushed ice. Blend on "low" speed for a few

seconds. Turn machine off and mix with a rubber scraper or spatula. Then blend a few more seconds and turn off the machine. Repeat until the ice is gone and the mixture is smooth. Eat immediately. If the blender seems to be working too hard, add a few extra drops of water.

This counts as ½ of your daily milk allowance and 1 fruit. It can be eaten any time.

Variations: Add 1 cap of brandy extract when using a peach. Also, why not try using ¼ of a pineapple as fruit.

ICE CREAM IN ORANGE SHELL

1 orange
Peach Ice Cream (p. 171)

Cut 1″ off the end of an orange. With a sharp paring knife, cut away the fruit from the shell and then remove. Cut the top of the orange shell in inverted "V's" (like "saw-tooth" all around the top). If the shell does not stand by itself, cut a very small slice from the bottom. Be careful not to cut through the bottom. Fill orange shell with the Peach Ice Cream (Strawberry, Pineapple or Pistachio would be good, too). Place in the freezer for at least 1 hour or longer. Allow to thaw partially before serving.

Remember to count the ice cream and fruit toward your daily allowances.

Variation: You can use a grapefruit shell, if you wish. Cut the grapefruit in half and proceed with the recipe as given.

ORANGE CREAMSICLE

6 ozs. of buttermilk
6 ozs. of Cott's Diet Orange Soda
1 to 2 envelopes of Sweet 'N Low, to taste

Mix all of the above together and pour into molds. Freeze until solid.

Try using orange juice instead of the orange soda, if you don't mind using some of your daily fruit allowance. Remember to count the buttermilk toward your daily milk allowance.

Beverages

If using the daily milk allowance is difficult, try my Continental Coffee, or any of the other beverages in this section.

You might also enjoy making ice cream with your milk (pp. 171-176).

Milk may also be used in preparing creamed soups—especially good in cold weather!

WAYS WITH MILK

A. Use dry skimmed milk crystals directly in your coffee or tea. If the coffee has been boiled, wait for one minute before adding.

B. Sweeten buttermilk with Sweet 'N Low to taste, and use over sliced peaches or blueberries.

C. Mix cottage cheese with cut-up radishes, cucumbers and scallions. Thin the cottage cheese first with several tablespoons of buttermilk. Add salt and pepper to taste.

D. Make a milk shake by adding dry skimmed milk crystals to diet soda; then add the ice.

E. Use evaporated skimmed milk, skimmed milk crystals or liquified skimmed milk, to make creamed soups.

F. Use milk in making ice cream (pp. 171-175) or a creamsicle, which is very good (p. 176).

G. Mix half buttermilk, half tomato juice, salt and pepper to taste, and a sprinkling of chives. Serve over ice cubes.

H. Mix half buttermilk, half diet orange soda and a little Sweet 'N Low (to taste). Serve over ice cubes.

BRANDY ALEXANDER

⅓ cup of powdered milk
¼ cup of cream or coffee diet soda
1 cap of vanilla extract
1 cap of brandy extract
2 ice cubes
½ envelope of Sweet 'N Low
Nutmeg

Blend all of the ingredients, except the nutmeg. Then sprinkle the nutmeg on top.

This is ½ of your daily milk allowance!

CONTINENTAL COFFEE

1 cup of skimmed milk
1 tsp. of instant coffee
½ cinnamon stick, or more
1 envelope Sweet 'N Low

Bring the milk, instant coffee and cinnamon to a boil. Allow to cool slightly. Add 1 envelope, or more, of the sweetener . . . and enjoy! (Remove the cinnamon stick before serving.)

Each cup is ½ of daily milk allowance.

If you want to make four servings, increase the ingredients as follows:

4 cups of skimmed milk
4 tsps. of instant coffee
1 cinnamon stick
3-4 envelopes Sweet 'N Low

CINNAMON MILK

1 cup of skim milk
½ cinnamon stick
1 envelope of Sweet 'N Low

Bring the cinnamon stick and milk to a boil. Add sweetener to taste. Remove the cinnamon stick before serving.

Be sure to count the milk toward your daily allowance.

LAZY GAL'S ICED TEA

½ gallon bottle of cold water
4 to 5 Lipton tea bags
Lemon juice and sweetener, to taste

Place the tea bags in the bottle of cold water and cover. Refrigerate for several hours, or overnight. When the tea is the desired strength, remove the tea bags and add lemon juice and sweetener. Serve over ice cubes.

This, of course, is unlimited . . . and it's so easy. It will keep in the refrigerator for several days without becoming cloudy.

FRESCA COOLER

4 ozs. of Fresca Diet Soda
4 ozs. of orange juice
Sprigs of mint
Ice cubes

Mix the soda and orange juice together; then add the ice cubes. Garnish with sprigs of mint.

Count 4 ozs. of orange juice as one fruit.

ORANGE-BUTTERMILK COOLER

4 ozs. of orange diet soda
4 ozs. of buttermilk
½ to 1 envelope of Sweet 'N Low

Mix all of the above ingredients together and refrigerate until chilled. Serve with ice.

Remember to count the milk toward your daily allowance.

INDEX

Index